THE

DEVIANT'S

Pocket Guide to the Outlandish Sexual Desires
Barely Contained in Your Subconscious

This is a work of humor. The sexual deviances and the information about them are real, but some facts may have been omitted because the author holds latent tendencies that made reporting on certain details prohibitively uncomfortable. This is not to be used as a medical text.

The Deviant's Pocket Guide is produced by becker&mayer! books, Bellevue, Washington www.beckermayer.com

Copyright © 2008 by Dennis DiClaudio

Published by Bloomsbury USA, New York
Distributed to the trade by Holtzbrinck Publishers

All papers used by Bloomsbury USA are natural, recyclable products made from wood grown in well-managed forests. The manufacturing processes conform to the environmental regulations of the country of origin.

Cataloging-in-Publication Data is available from the Library of Congress.

ISBN 1-59691-409-2
ISBN-13 978-1-59691-409-4

First U.S. Edition 2008

10 9 8 7 6 5 4 3 2 1

Cover design by Bryan Danknich.

Printed in China by SNP Leefung Printers Limited.

THE
DEVIANT'S

Pocket Guide to the Outlandish Sexual Desires
Barely Contained in Your Subconscious

DENNIS DICLAUDIO

BLOOMSBURY

CONTENTS

FANTASYLAND

FLORA & FAUNA

COSTUMES & PLAY

INTRODUCTION

Ever since Barry White invented sex in 1961, people have been asking, "Is that all there is?"

Yes, the procreative act, or break dancing on the good sheets, as you may call it, is pretty fun the first eight or nine times you try it, but it gets old in a hurry. *You lie down here, and I'll do this, and watch out because I don't think that's supposed to bend back that far. Goddamnit, the cat's watching us again. Go away, Buckles. Mommy and Daddy are busy doing grown-up people stuff right now. Go play with your squeaky mouse.*

You might be relieved to know that no, in fact, that's not all there is. There are pioneers out there who have made amazing and wondrous advances in sex. Who have pushed the human libido to its very limits and then slapped it and made it call them "Professor Daddy." Thanks to their noble efforts, we now know that pain can be a good thing, given the proper context. We know that chocolate pudding is not just for eating. We know that clowns are not always creepy, that cold marble statues can make us hot, and that teddy bears can be specially modified for very special uses. And, perhaps most importantly, we know that "tree hugger" is not just a clever name.

Perhaps some of this strikes a chord. Maybe you thought you were the only person ever to feel erotically attracted to shrubbery. Or to fall hopelessly in love with a cartoon badger. Well, you're not. Not at all! No matter what your deepest secret fantasy might entail, a quick browse through an Internet search engine will relieve you of any misconceptions of loneliness.

When I began writing this book, I was actually a little concerned that there might not be enough information available on sexual deviancies to support an entire volume. My concerns were quickly put to rest; however, I did need to modify my tactics slightly from how I approached my two previous *Pocket Guides*. As it turns out, while there are plenty of people willing to talk (in detail) about their particular kinks, there simply aren't a lot of licensed sexologists publishing papers on erotic enemas. So I do hope you'll forgive me if I write about gentlemen squeezing vinegar onto ladies' bathing suit areas with a slightly less scientific bent than I would ordinarily prefer.

The forty-two sexual deviancies detailed here are really just the tip of the bull-whip—there's so much more for you to learn. The sources I found myself turning to over and over again were Brenda Love's *Encyclopedia of Unusual Sex Practices*, Katharine Gates's *Deviant Desires*, and Dan Savage's newspaper advice column *Savage Love*. All three are highly entertaining and informative. I couldn't recommend any of them more highly without running the risk of alienating friends and family. Even more.

—*Dennis J. DiClaudio, Jr., B.A.*

PRETTY PAIN

BDSM
(ALSO BONDAGE & DISCIPLINE, DOMINATION & SUBMISSION, SADISM & MASOCHISM, SADOMASOCHISM)

The pleasure of the right kind of pain.

USEFUL ACCOUTREMENTS

- leather
- chains
- whips
- gags
- clamps
- bindings
- cuffs
- What else you got?

THE FANTASY

You find the ad in the back pages:

"SWM seeks SWF for meaningful relationship. Should appreciate art, literature, and classical music, enjoy cooking together, traveling, discussing politics, beating with canes, stepping on faces, cutting, biting, bleeding, binding, berating, humiliating, smacking, slapping, spanking, choking, suffocating, punching, pushing, kicking, burning, electrocuting, waterboarding, and

locking partners in the closet for hours on end
because they're such naughty, naughty boys. Having
your own butt plug is a plus. No smokers please."

And you live happily ever after.

WHAT IS IT?

It's practically impossible to talk about most sexual fetishes without first touching upon BDSM (Bondage & Discipline, Sadism & Masochism). And that's all you really *can*
do: touch upon it. To attempt to fully explain its various
incarnations and nuances would require several volumes,
a sturdy oak shelf, a whip, some handcuffs, and two (possibly three) leather-clad volunteers. It truly is the *Sgt. Pepper* of sexual fetishes: It may not have come first, but its
roots go way back to the beginning, and it has influenced
everything since. BDSM is also a comforting fetish to return to after getting tired of all the fancy newer stuff. It's
probably the most important thing to happen to sex since
the invention of the clitoris in 1965. And, whether you
know (or want to believe) it or not, you almost certainly
already engage in it to some degree. Unless you don't have
sex. And, even then, you probably still do.

You've likely seen BDSM on television or in movies
(when the writers are trying to make a character seem
weird without having to do any actual creative work). It often involves leather, bindings, cuffs, whips, or chains, but

it doesn't need to. In fact it doesn't need to involve props or special clothing at all. BDSM play can be as simple as one naked person seemingly treating another naked person very poorly, physically and/or psychologically. Or it can get much more complicated, as you'll see elsewhere in this book. But the one person is not actually being treated poorly. In a sense. BDSM is complicated.

At its heart, BDSM is the pleasure received by two people playing with status. One dominant and one submissive. A top and a bottom. Master and slave. Dithers and Bumstead. These are intentional roles, usually decided in advance, and they don't have to have anything to do with real-life status. In fact, they're often based on the inverse.

PSYCHOLOGICAL ORIGINS

There are so many reasons a person might get into BDSM, and it's an interest held by so many different types of people across so many walks of life, that it hardly makes sense to go into it in depth here. See all the other pages in this book for more specific explanations.

The most important thing to remember in any type of BDSM play is that the safety and comfort of you and your partner are paramount. BDSM might look dark and dangerous, but it's actually (or should be) consensual play between two people who respect one another. BDSM is not you unilaterally deciding to torture your partner, which is illegal. Both of you need to be completely on board. And don't ever do anything that could accidentally cause long-term bodily harm. Or death. Death is even worse.

Many BDSM fetishists establish a "safe word," an agreed-upon term that signals all play must stop immediately. For example, if you're Egyptologists, you might choose "Neferneferuré." Then, if one of you is feeling unpleasantly uncomfortable or genuinely frightened by what's going on, you can just shout "Neferneferuré!" and your partner will know to stop. (You might choose something a little easier to pronounce.)

Of Note . . .

Leather and latex clothing was very closely associated with the BDSM subculture through decades in which fetishists were forced to keep their lifestyles secret. Now, pre-teens wear it to junior high school. Time has such a sick sense of humor.

CASTRATION FETISH

The sexual fantasy of throwing out your junk.

USEFUL ACCOUTREMENTS

- vodka
- antiseptic
- gauze
- scissors

THE FANTASY

She reenters the room with a sadistic gleam in her eye, and your muscles inadvertently recoil. The rope tightens around your wrists. Your mouth is dry; you can feel your heart beating heavily beneath your breastbone. She approaches you on the bed and lays the chainsaw gentle beside your leg. The cold metal of its bar falls against your bare flesh.

"So sad to say goodbye to something so pretty," she says. You close your eyes and roll your head backward. You feel the release of weight as she lifts the chainsaw from the bed. In the moment's quiet, you can hear your own heartbeat. And then she pulls the starting cord. The saw sputters a few times, then goes quiet. She pulls the cord again. And again. "Um," she says, "how do I work this?"

"Is the choke in the on position?" you say.

"What's a choke?" she says.

WHAT IS IT?

From the moment a male infant discovers the organ dangling precariously between his legs, his mind becomes transfixed on a single thought: "How can I get rid of this thing?" As he ages and grows into a healthy boy, the appendage grows with him. "Perhaps," he thinks, "it will eventually fall off on its own." In most cases, no such luck. Rather, it becomes more prominent, demanding attention at the playground or in the middle of history class. Its appetite, it seems, is insatiable. "Go into the garage," it demands. "Find that stack of magazines."

Soon it forces the boy out of his bedroom and into school-sponsored dance parties. It leads the boy into the backseat of cars, the underside of bleachers and the bedrooms of friends' parents who are away for the weekend. "My God," the boy thinks, "this monster must be stopped!" It is then that the boy begins fantasizing about drastic steps. Ways to rid himself of this problem—for good.

The man who is steadfast and courageous enough to follow through with his overwhelming desire for castration is rare. Biology, psychology, and society have conspired against him. The mind does not want to lose an organ it deems crucial to the propagation of the species. Laws have been put in place making it illegal to surgically remove a man's genitals without good reason. But while some men are content to act out their castration fixation through fantasy—toy cleavers, breakaway cords, and other things not available at Toys 'R' Us—the dedicated man persists. He tracks down sadomasochism dungeons or underground castration clinics—such as the one recently busted near Waynesville, North Carolina—that are sympathetic to his desires. And he does what needs to be done.

Others, lacking in moral fiber, eventually submit to a more socially acceptable and symbolic form of castration: Marriage.

"My God," the boy thinks, "this monster must be stopped!"

PSYCHOLOGICAL ORIGINS

If you're not one of those people who want nothing more than to have your member's membership revoked, this may all seem pretty silly and confounding. Why would anybody want to do this to himself? It could be that the man in question is disgusted by sex or by the kind of sex he desires. For example, a recidivistic sex offender who wants to change his ways may view this as a last source of hope. Alternatively, for a man who greatly fears a loss of manhood, the fear itself may become sexually charged. So stepping closer and closer to the fear actually becomes erotically stimulating.

As with the Crush Fetish (page 130), to have the locus of your sexuality destroyed by a dominant woman may be the ultimate form of submissiveness.

CASTRATION FETISH

CONSIDERATIONS

Here's the thing, if castration is your thing: You can really only do it the once. So you'd better make certain you enjoy yourself that one time. After losing your penis and/or scrotum, you'll most likely experience decreased mental acuity and loss of muscle mass, body strength, and body hair due to decreased testosterone. You may also find yourself more depressed than usual (which probably isn't that hard to believe).

What you may want to do to experiment with castration (try before you buy, if you will) is inject yourself with Depo-Provera, a drug prescribed to sex offenders. It'll pretty much achieve the same results as a physical castration, except that it wears off.

However, castration in any form is not recommended. If castration is genuinely in your fantasies, you should probably keep it there. There are all sorts of ways that you and your partner can play with pretend-castration (plastic knives, role-playing, fake blood, etc.). The great thing about this kind of castration is that you can do it every night!

Here's the thing, if castration is your thing: You can really only do it the once. So you'd better enjoy yourself that one time.

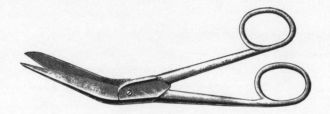

Of Note . . .

Castration of one or both testicles may sometimes be necessary for medical reasons, such as testicular or prostate cancer. Because the adrenal glands also produce testosterone, the sex drive may not be lost completely. While orgasms may be achieved with more difficulty, they are still possible.

CUCKOLDRY

The desire to have another man take your wife, please take her.

USEFUL ACCOUTREMENTS

- comfy chair
- good sight lines
- some dude

THE FANTASY

Having spent a long day working your ass off at your crappy job and fighting your way through rush-hour traffic, you're elated to finally pull into your cul-de-sac. Slowing to a crawl, you pull the car up to a stretch of curb hidden from your house by a large maple and cut the engine. Leaving briefcase and coat on the passenger seat, you ease out of the cabin and make your way stealthily across the street and over the side lawn, pausing just briefly to take in the sleek lines of the unfamiliar silver Porsche parked in the driveway. A Porsche—you should have known.

The side door is unlocked, so you quietly ease open the knob and slip into the dark kitchen. Certain she doesn't know you're home, you tiptoe across the dark kitchen and up the back stairs, picking up a faint sound coming from the master bedroom. A steady creak of metal on metal. As you near the landing, other noises become audible: Heavy breathing. A woman's moans. An occasional man's grunt. Oh, she's bad. She's *very* bad.

Reaching the bedroom, you pause and take a breath to calm your quickened pulse. As you throw open the door, your wife looks up from the bed.

"Take a seat, hon."

"Great, but next time wait until I get home, would you?" you say, settling into a chair. "At least give me a chance to make popcorn."

WHAT IS IT?

Here's something to think about: Right now, there are thousands—if not millions—of men out there who would be more than willing to do every dirty thing to your wife that you can dream up. They're bigger than you, stronger than you, more virile than you. Their hair is thick and their bellies don't blebb over the waistbands of their underwear (which is clean and neatly pressed). Your wife will love it. She'll love them. She'll scream in delight and moan in ecstasy in a way you've never heard before. Her eyes will roll back in their sockets and her knuckles will turn white as she clutches feverishly at the bed sheets.

And, if you like, you can sit in the corner of the room and watch. Make yourself comfortable and enjoy the show. After all, this is what you wanted. You orchestrated it, in fact. You spent weeks begging your wife to consider taking another man into your bed. You found the other man—or "stud," as they're called in Cuckoldry circles and 1970s softcore porn films—on one of those websites (it might have been *Cuckold World*, or was it *Housewife Bangers*?) and asked him to meet you and your wife for a drink. So now, after all your efforts, you can finally sit back, relax, and take in the sweet humiliation of watching your beautiful wife—or "hotwife"—and another man turn you into a "cuck."

You may think that this is a new phenomenon, but it's not. This sort of thing has been going on for years, probably as long as people have had wives to be humiliated by. Appropriately enough, Leopold von Sacher-Masoch, the French novelist for whom Masochism was named, used to beg his wife to humiliate him in such a fashion. And, so disappointed was he that she refused, that their marriage eventually folded. Some guys just really need a good "cucking."

> Make yourself comfortable
> and enjoy the show. After all,
> you orchestrated it.

PSYCHOLOGICAL ORIGINS

Humiliation is the primary force behind most cases of Cuckoldry. In this sense, it's similar to many types of BDSM play, with the "cuck" in the submissive role while the "hotwife" and "stud" co-play the dominant. But this is often misleading. In many cases, the "cuck," though seemingly being subjugated, is the one calling the shots, conducting from the orchestra pit, so to speak. For whatever reason, he's getting off on the humiliation, possibly because a fear of being cheated upon has become fetishized in his mind.

Or, this may be a way for him to realize certain latent homosexual fantasies. Although he may not want to have sex with another man, he may actually want to have sex with another man. Through Cuckoldry he's able to vicariously experience his fantasies via his wife. Kind of.

As for your wife and her new sexual friend, they're probably having fun, too. They're the ones having sex anyway, right? Your wife may be into humiliating you as much as you're into being humiliated. And the "stud" gets to feel like an alpha male. It's a huge ego stroke to walk into a couple's bedroom and please a woman like her man could never hope to.

CONSIDERATIONS

For some couples, the excitement of living out a Cuckoldry fantasy can actually be a revitalizing force for their sex life and relationship. But both parties have to be into it. If you force your partner's hand, it could very easily lead to trust issues and, ultimately, the dissolution of your relationship. If you're gonna do something like this, talk about it first. And then talk about it some more.

Of Note . . .

Certain species of Cuckoo bird, from which the word "cuckold" is derived, make a habit laying their eggs in the nests of other birds. The unsuspecting bird will care for the eggs as though they are its own. Once the eggs hatch and the gullible nurturer realizes its mistake, a deep feeling of shame and pathos will descend upon it. The species most commonly preyed upon by the Cuckoo include the European Sissytail and the Brown-headed Pantywaist.

DACRYPHILIA

The crying game.

USEFUL ACCOUTREMENTS

○ Kleenex
○ sentimental disposition
○ *Steel Magnolias*
○ *Old Yeller*
○ that one episode of *Sesame Street* when Mr. Hooper died

THE FANTASY

Just hold her. Hold her so close to your breast as the tears roll down her face that she can feel the warmth of your body deep inside hers. Deep inside her soul. Make her feel safe. Let her know that you will always be here for her when she is overcome with sadness and pain.

Wow, she's really letting it out. This might be the hardest you've ever seen her cry. Her cheeks are sopping wet. She must have been deeply hurt. She must be in so much pain. Thank God you're here for her when she needs you most! Where are those tissues?

There they are, next to the studded leather blackjack you were using to beat her ankles.

WHAT IS IT?

Most people think of crying as an emotional response to sadness, pain, or not being able to figure out how to change the ring tone on their cell phones. But for a certain subset of the BDSM community, crying is a powerful aphrodisiac. For Dacryphiliacs, there is nothing quite so stimulating as watching their partner fall into tears before them. Except maybe falling into tears themselves. And they'll often seek out such experiences.

But it's not really a one-tear-fits-all type of situation. A Dacryphiliac who gets off on watching his partner cry from humiliation or ridicule may not enjoy it when his or her partner cries from genuine sadness or pain. And one who likes tears of joy may not like tears of humiliation at all. And nobody, not even Dacryphiliacs, like the kind of tears that come streaming from obnoxiously loud women at funerals, church sermons, or sappy movies. (Everyone gets it; you're the saddest person in the room. Now shut up.)

Similarly, the desired response can be variable. A Dacryphiliac who berates his partner for crying may want to comfort her immediately afterwards, but she might not want that comfort at all. She might want to be berated further, to more furious tears. And another Dacryphiliac may want nothing more than to have his partner hold him through his lamentations, while his partner may take that as his cue to start unbuckling his pants. Or simply inducing the tears might have been the highlight of the experience for him, and now he just wants to watch some football.

PSYCHOLOGICAL ORIGINS

There are a number of factors that may draw you to Dacryphilia. If you're the crier (the submissive), you may enjoy the feeling of total emotional nakedness that crying affords. Or you may be seeking the emotional release, which can be very powerful. Many doctors believe that the act of crying causes the body to release endorphins into the blood stream that act as mood-elevators or pain relievers. So crying can produce an effect that is not dissimilar to using mood-altering drugs.

If you like to induce the crying, it may actually stem from a psychological desire to care for your partner. By moving him or her to tears, you are creating a scenario in which you get to switch gears and step in as the comforter. It's a sort of odd, roundabout way of achieving your goal, but if it works for you, whatever.

Or you might just be a sadist. There's plenty of room for sadists in the world of sex.

PRETTY PAIN

CONSIDERATIONS

If you're going to embark upon some Dacryphilia play, you should definitely make certain that your partner is into it as well. That sort of emotional tinkering is not something with which everyone is comfortable. And making your partner cry without his or her consent, or even back-dooring your way into making him or her make you cry, is kind of sadistic. But not in the good BDSM kind of way.

Of Note . . .

Although it is commonly believed that humans are the only animal sophisticated enough to cry, there is some evidence that elephants may also have the capacity. There is, however, no evidence that they have a sophisticated enough sense of gettin'-it-on to make the leap to Dacryphilia.

MEDICAL FETISH

The prescription for specialized loving care.

USEFUL ACCOUTREMENTS

- latex gloves
- tongue depressor
- warming salve
- tight bandages
- rectal thermometer
- therapeutic dildo

THE FANTASY

Good lord! This is the most advanced case of aggravated hotness of the booty you've seen in years. You need to get this patient undressed, lubed-up, and facedown on the operating table immediately! There's no time for scrubbing—you'll just have to start operating like the dirty doctor you are.

Blood pulse is up. Breathing heavy and erratic. Where's that damned nurse with the nipple clamps? You're losing her! You'll need to administer 200 CCs of pelvic thrusting, *stat!*

WHAT IS IT?

To quote a completely made up statistic from a study that never actually occurred, 53.7 percent of all children play

"Doctor" at some point in their childhood (while only 0.008 percent play "Statistician"). For children, it's an opportunity to explore the bodies of themselves and their playmates, a way to experiment with their burgeoning sexuality within a context they can understand, and a chance to really freak out their overprotective parents.

While most kids grow past this exciting, though ultimately harmless, practice and move on to more mature forms of sexual expression (such as "Pretending You're Satisfied" and "Withholding Until He Apologizes"), there are a small number (7 percent? Why not?) who stick with it, or who rediscover the game as an adult. These people have graduated into the world of the Medical Fetish.

To the discerning Medical Fetishist, the fantasy is much more nuanced than simply having sex while wearing a white coat and one of those reflective headband things. It's a somewhat precise form of play-acting that involves actual doctorial understanding and, in some cases, an impressive collection of equipment. In many scenarios, one partner playing the role of the (submissive) patient will enter the examining room of the (dominant) doctor and will be ordered to remove his or her clothing. The doctor will then poke and prod with various instruments, thoroughly handle the breasts and/or genitals, and perhaps request a semen (or vaginal secretion) sample. Bandaging or splinting may be in order. In some cases, an enema might even be administered (see Klismaphilia, page 52). Sometimes it's just a matter of good old-fashioned sexual healing.

The more convincingly a scene is played, regardless of how improbable it may seem, the more erotic it tends to be for both parties. In many cases, no actual sex need occur. The serious Medical Fetish aficionado may create a rather convincing examination room and fill it with such medical toys as forceps, dental mouth gags, speculums, catheters, and items so spiked and studded that if your real doctor ever pulled them on you, you'd likely faint.

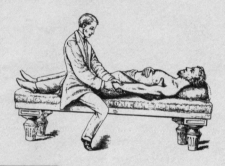

PSYCHOLOGICAL ORIGINS

For many Medical Fetishists, the pleasure derives either from being naked and submissive before an authority figure, or from dominating a naked person who must comply with his or her every "professional" whim. The fetish may also be born from unexpected excitement found during a genuine medical examination.

Some people are moved to add light surgery to their Medical Fetish. As with any activity that involves even minor bloodletting, immense precautions must be taken. While this kind of thing is not recommended, if you are dead-set upon doing it, make sure both you and your partner are comfortable with everything that will occur, use only sterile instruments, and by all means, establish a safe word.

Of Note . . .

While similar to—and possibly symptomatic of—the Medical Fetish, Iatronudia deserves to be identified as its own fetish, characterized by the sexual pleasure derived from being unclothed before a genuine medical professional. In its benign state, it can simply be a small thrill felt during a necessary examination, thus rendering the procedure more pleasant. However, if consistent with the mental disorder Munchausen Syndrome (please refer to the previous volume, *The Paranoid's Pocket Guide*, Bloomsbury 2007), it may manifest as the repeated feigning of symptoms for the express purpose of undressing in front of a doctor. In this case, Iatronudia may be seen as a drain upon medical time and expenses.

TELEPHONE SCATALOGIA

(ALSO TELEPHONICOPHILIA)

The pleasure of bothering people when they're just sitting down to dinner.

USEFUL ACCOUTREMENTS

- cordless phone
- discount long distance provider
- intimacy issues

THE FANTASY

There's something in the timbre of her voice that makes you all aflutter. Words fail you. Your mind goes blank. But you desperately need to express these feelings that have kept your heart swollen since the first time she said *hello*. You need just the right phrase . . . the exact poetry of syllables and meter . . .

Pacing the living room with the telephone clutched tightly in your fist, you push your mind to think. Think, damn you! *Meretricious*? No, that sounds like you're trying too hard. You need something simple and elegant and to the point.

You're a filthy whore. Yes! That's it!

With a hungry heart, you unbuckle your pants and dial the phone.

WHAT IS IT?

What are you wearing? Are you in your underwear? Are you naked? Where are you reading this book? In your bed? In the bathroom? You're dirty, aren't you? You probably like being called dirty, don't you? Or do you like to call random people and tell them they are? If so, then you're into Telephone Scatalogia.

That's the more clinical way of saying obscene phone calls. Different people go about their Telephone Scatalogia in different ways. You've got your verbal abusers. You've got your naughty confessors (kinda like telephone exhibitionists). Then there are the immediate-hang-uppers, generally the most cowardly type. There are the heavy breathers—they're fun. (Not to be confused with genuine asthmatics.) But then there are the really clever obscene callers. They'll trick you into a conversation that seems banal and then slowly ramp up the dirtiness ("You know, you can put chocolate sauce on just about *anything* . . . ") or get you to start revealing intimate information ("So, what's your social security number?"). What they all have in common is that they do "things" to their "selves" during or immediately after the call.

PSYCHOLOGICAL ORIGINS

Most Telephone Scatalogists suffer from anger and/or intimacy issues, which keep them from forming real life relationships with real life people. Some also have a deep need to communicate, to feel close to somebody, and since they can't do it in person, they resort to the phone. Others just want to yank it to the sound of your voice.

CONSIDERATIONS

Have you heard of caller ID? Yeah, lots of people have that nowadays, and it'll kinda put a kink in your "anonymous" phone call fun. And even if the person you're dialing doesn't, the telephone company keeps a record of all calls that go through its wires. So if somebody really wants to catch you—like if you're dumb enough to keep calling the same person over and over again—it's not hard to do.

Enrolling yourself in some sessions of behavioral therapy to boost your self-esteem and kick the Telephone Scatalogia habit is probably a good idea. There are better ways for you to live out your sex life. Ways that are far less annoying to other people.

Of Note . . .

Not all instances of Telephone Scatalogia are intentional. A small percentage of obscene phone calls occur completely by accident. Suppose, for example, you were writing a book about strange sex habits and you got a phone call from someone you *thought* was your friend Jessica, and you said something like, "I just spent the past four hours writing about having sex with trees," but then it turned out it wasn't your friend Jessica, it was actually a wrong number. Please, please be aware that the person speaking in this type of scenario would in no way be trying to get off, if any people like the caller happen to be reading this book.

BODIES, PARTS & FUNCTIONS

ACROTOMOPHILIA

The feeling that their loss is your gain.

USEFUL ACCOUTREMENTS

- ○ lack of arm
- ○ lack of leg
- ○ lack of other arm
- ○ lack of other leg

THE FANTASY

Look at him. He's gorgeous. Perfectly tousled hair, sparkly eyes, big manly hands, iron jaw. And his body is great, really great, but . . . well, if he could just lose five or ten pounds. You know, in the lower leg. Say, from the knee down. Oh, that would be so hot. Hell, even if he was just missing a foot . . .

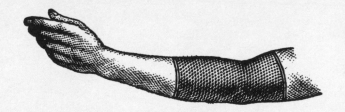

Close your eyes and try to imagine your perfect sexual partner. Do your best to really visual every feature and curve. Do you have a mental picture? Great. Now, quick: How many limbs does this person have? If you answered three or fewer, you might want to look into Acrotomophilia.

Acrotomophiliacs are drawn to amputees. They go crazy over the shapely nubs that suggest arms and legs that used to be. There's magic in the minus—just think of all the things you could do with an amputated limb. Or what it could do to you.

The problem you face as an Acrotomophiliac is that there really aren't a ton of amputees on the dating market. Unless you work in a veteran's hospital or a lion tamer's academy, you're not likely to run into someone who really tickles your fancy. Some Acrotomophiles do take proactive steps like attending—and sometimes even organizing—disability support group meetings and events, hoping to attract their "type."

PSYCHOLOGICAL ORIGINS

For many Acrotomophiliacs, their sexual attraction to missing limbs actually comes from an *aversion* to missing limbs. The human sex drive is a complex thing, and often (as you'll find to be a recurring explanation for vaguely creepy sexual preferences) people's attractions spring from fear.

It could be that, as a child, your mother forced you to be nice to your Uncle Sy who lost both his legs in the war. So you trained yourself to look up, away from his lap, keeping your eyes locked firmly on his while he quizzed you with math questions several grades beneath your own, all the while feeling those two amputated limbs calling to you from his wheelchair seat. And perhaps those same limbs followed you into your dreams at night. And as you got older, you developed a fear of that kind of awkwardness. Or a fear that your disrespectful fear would condemn you to a fate similar to Uncle Sy's. Over time, maybe that fear slowly evolved into something exciting, something . . . sexual. And before you know it you're showing up to a family reunion with a former construction worker who once had an I-beam land on his legs, and your little niece is forced to be nice to him and train herself to look up, away from his lap, keeping her eyes locked firmly on his while he quizzes her with math questions several grades beneath her own.

You're not likely to run into someone who really tickles your fancy.

Regardless of how much you're genuinely attracted to amputees, you should understand that many amputees aren't interested in having what they perceive as their disability objectified and eroticized. Many amputees have not come to terms with their loss; not having a limb, for them, is not kinky, and they may not be able to understand why it is for you. So try to be mindful of their feelings. And, seriously, reconsider that stale "You must have phantom limbs, 'cause you've been running through my dreams *all* night!" pick-up line.

Of Note . . .

Apotemnophilia, or Body Integrity Identity Disorder, is a rare mental disorder in which a person desires to have perfectly functioning body parts amputated. Many Acrotomophiliacs are also Apotemnophiles and vice versa. (For more about Apotemnophilia, please refer to page 198 of *The Paranoid's Pocket Guide*, Bloomsbury 2007, or consult your local illegal black market surgery expert.)

EMETOPHILIA
(ALSO VOMEROPHILIA, ROMAN SHOWERS, RAINBOW SHOWERS, EROTIC VOMITING)

The sexual attraction to the regurgitated contents of a person's stomach.

USEFUL ACCOUTREMENTS

○ nausea
○ motion sickness

○ hangover
○ stomach flu

THE FANTASY

You always kind of suspected he had eyes for you. You could feel his gaze caressing your calves as you sat cross-legged by his desk and took notes. And he did seem to call you into his office slightly more than was necessary. Now, in the middle of the office holiday party, he's leaning in closely, confiding in you about his loveless marriage. You can smell the scotch thick on his breath. He's had too much to drink; he's being too forward.

He's attractive in an avuncular sort of way. Just a bit of gray to his immaculately combed-back hair. A kind face. Not the type you usually go for. But you like the attention he pays. He smiles gratefully at you and pulls the glass to his lips. As the liquor goes down, his face suddenly changes. It tinges green. His lips purse. He looks around, panicked, for a garbage pail, and then tips forward toward your lap and barfs everywhere.

Man, this guy is *hot*.

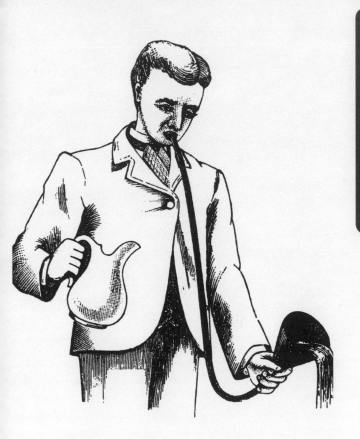

WHAT IS IT?

Surely, you relate to the tense excitement of exigent pressure building, aching deep within your body. The thrill that courses through your limbs, the feeling of sanguine tranquility in which you find yourself submerged immediately following the release. But do you usually need to brush your teeth afterwards?

Emetophilia is arousal via puke. It may entail getting off by watching somebody else vomit, or getting off by your own vomiting. It can be incredibly, incredibly gross under some circumstances and only very gross under others. Regardless, the star of the show is human emesis.

PSYCHOLOGICAL ORIGINS

It has been speculated that Emetophilia grows from a childhood fear of vomiting, or from a bad experience with it. As with many other fetishes, strong associated emotions can evolve into sexual associations. This theory is lent some credence by the seemingly counterintuitive fact that many Emetophiles are also Emeto*phobic*. (Human sexuality is a lovely and complex flower, is it not?)

Before engaging in an Emetophilic behavior during the physical act of love, you should clear it with your sexual partner first. Though you may worry that whispering "I'm going to upchuck on your face now" may dampen the heat of the moment, rest assured that it won't be nearly such a buzz-kill as what might happen if you barf on someone who *doesn't* think it's sexy.

Of Note . . .

Roman Showers—so named for the Romans' predilection for purging—seem to be particularly popular with the Sadomasochism set (see BDSM, page 10), as a quick hunt around the Internet will reveal. However, the Emetophilic purity of many vomit-oriented S&M scenarios is questionable, as it is often used primarily as a form of humiliation, with a dominant partner vomiting onto a submissive.

EPROCTOPHILIA
(ALSO FLATUPHILIA)

The infatuation with the flurry that flows forth from the fundament.

USEFUL ACCOUTREMENTS

- beans
- beans
- beans
- other musical fruits

THE FANTASY

"Aren't these speed-dating things weird?"

"Yeah. I always feel so awkward. I never know what to say."

"Me too. I'm just certain I'm gonna say—"

"—the wrong thing. Exactly. So, tell me about yourself."

"Well, I'm a marketing consultant by day. I play classical guitar and indoor soccer. Not at the same time."

"Ha."

"And I love farting. I love it! There's nothing I enjoy more than squatting down in front of somebody's face and ripping a nice strong smelly one."

"No way!"

"Yes way!"

"I love that too! There's nothing in the world that turns me on like inhaling a woman's repugnant effluvia!"

"Oh, that's such a nice way of putting it. Tell me more about yourself."

WHAT IS IT?

Flatulence is primarily nitrogen, methane, and hydrogen that build up in your lower intestines from the air you breathe and as a byproduct of digesting food. The accompanying smell is a result of the butyric acid, hydrogen sulfide, and carbonyl sulfide that it contains in smaller amounts. To many people, this combination of factors is disgusting. To others, it's hilarious. To the Eproctophiliac, it is lovely beyond words.

Eproctophiliacs desire nothing so much as to have you fart. Sometimes, they just want to hear it. Sometimes they want to watch you fart. Sometimes they want to fart on you, or have you fart on them. In any case, it's all just a part of the courting process. Some couples drink wine and eat cheese, and some couples ass-whine and cut cheese.

PSYCHOLOGICAL ORIGINS

Eproctophilia may be a slightly tamer version of Coprophilia (the sexual attraction to feces), or it may be a form of Sadomasochism (see BDSM, page 10). It is generally believed that it derives from a desire to debase or to be debased on some level. Certainly there is an element of humiliation involved.

If you're going to indulge in Eproctophilic behavior, don't do it near an open fire, as the methane and hydrogen contained in flatulence are flammable, and one unlucky fart could cause some serious singeing. And don't be stingy with your farts while waiting for Mr. or Mrs. Right. Holding them in may lead to constipation. Relax, there'll be more where those came from.

Of Note . . .

Irish author James Joyce was believed to have been an Eproctophiliac. At any rate, he sure liked writing about farts, as evidenced by the dirty letters he wrote to his wife, Nora: "You had an arse full of farts that night, darling . . . big fat fellows, long windy ones, quick little merry cracks and a lot of tiny little naughty farties ending in a long gush from your hole . . . I think I would know Nora's fart anywhere. I think I could pick hers out in a roomful of farting women . . . I hope Nora will let off no end of her farts in my face so that I may know their smell also."

No, seriously, he did.

KLISMAPHILIA

The pleasure of purging the bowels.

USEFUL ACCOUTREMENTS

- lubricant
- nozzle
- bag
- water
- drainage tube

THE FANTASY

He's very handsome. There's no denying his uncanny good looks. And he's witty. And smart. And he certainly does know his way around a wine list. You find yourself wondering, is he truly the one? The one you've been waiting for all these years? Or is he just another waste of your time?

The cab is getting close to your apartment. You'll have to decide soon. You're through with depressing one-night stands, which somehow always leave you feeling dirty. You don't want to feel dirty anymore. You want someone who will make you feel clean. Who will flush out all the rotten perspectives of yourself, and make you feel unspoiled and fresh. He could be the one. The cab is pulling to a halt; you're home. The time has come to ask.

You turn to him, toss back your hair, bat your eyelashes.

"Would you like to come upstairs for a drink," you ask, "and then stick a rubber tube up my ass?"

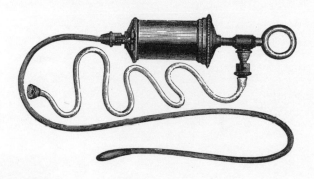

WHAT IS IT?

Over the years, mankind has made great strides in discovering new and exciting things to stick up its butt. Sextants, light bulbs, car keys, flash drives. They all have their individual charms, but something—some sort of innate spiritual hunger, perhaps—continues to lure man back to the most basic of ingredients: water.

Klismaphilia, the sexual enjoyment of receiving or administering enemas, is certainly the most Taoist of fetishes. The experience of filling your lower intestine with water is a powerful one. Water is as yielding as it is forceful. It maintains no permanent shape of its own and, therefore, can occupy all available cavity space. When it encounters a blockage, it simply bypasses it, cleansing and flushing on its way. It can be cool and refreshing or warm and soothing. Sure, people may enjoy mixing foreign elements into their enema water (coffee, wheatgrass, vodka, cocaine) for various added effects, but it is the water that is essential.

If you like, you and your partner can fold your enema-fun into BDSM by including a little spanking or other forms of role-playing (see Medical Fetish, page 30). And for people who aren't comfortable with expelling feces in front of a loved one, a pre-enema means any ensuing Klismaphilic activity is just good clean water sports.

PSYCHOLOGICAL ORIGINS

Klismaphilia feels good, which is probably a big factor in turning people onto it. The water and the enema nozzle stimulate the nerve endings of the anus and rectum in a manner similar to anal sex. For men, the water pressure on the prostate can also be very enjoyable. Enemas are also known to have many non-sexual healing effects. Coffee enemas, for example, are believed to be useful for detoxing the liver.

That said, why anyone would enjoy *administering* an enema is less obvious, but maybe folks think of it as paying their dues.

Be careful not to overfill the rectum with water. The average person can take in somewhere between one and three quarts, which should be administered slowly (approximately one cup per minute). Too much water pressure may cause injury. It's also a good idea not to share your enema tools.

If you have enemas too often—more than once every three days or so—you may become dependent upon the procedure for bowel movements. It's recommended that you study up on enema safety before becoming a full-time Klismaphiliac.

One important last note: The body absorbs chemicals faster through the walls of the rectum than through the stomach, so if you're thinking of adding anything like caffeine or alcohol to your enema solution, tread very carefully. Again, study up. Smart enema sex is safe enema sex.

Of Note . . .

King Louis XIV of France was a world-class enema fanatic. In his seventy-seven years, he reportedly enjoyed more than 2,000 enemas. He ruled for seventy-two years as one of the country's greatest, healthiest, and happiest kings.

LACTAPHILIA
(ALSO EROTIC LACTATION)

The need for the milk of human kindness.

USEFUL ACCOUTREMENTS

- O nipples
- O breasts
- O breast milk

THE FANTASY

The passengers on the bus are trying their best not to look, stealing quick, furtive glances at the young mother sitting across the aisle from you nursing her infant. But she continues to feed, her child sucking hungrily at her ample bosoms. She brushes a lock of long brown hair from her chest, revealing a small wet circle of milk on her shirt. She looks quickly from the stain to you, and your eyes dart to the floor. When you look up again, you notice that the baby is pawing at his mother, unwilling to continue his meal. The young woman turns to you and says with glimmering eyes, "Oh no. My baby is full, but I still have all this milk left inside me. Whatever shall I do?"

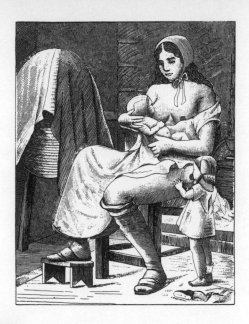

WHAT IS IT?

As an infant, you were treated to your first taste of breasts. They were your mother's, but you hadn't yet seen magazine underwear ads or watched Cinemax late night, so you weren't very discerning. At the time, they were all the breasts you knew in the world, and you were happy for them. They represented warmth, safety, and comfort, they made this strange feeling of "hunger" go away—they were pretty much the best things ever. Then you got older and started playing with Tonka trucks and My Pretty Ponies and sort of forgot about breasts for a while.

Or maybe you didn't. Maybe you got older and kept that memory of suckling at your mother's breast close to your heart. Maybe as you reached puberty, your desire moved down from your heart and into your pants. Maybe when you lost your virginity in the shrubs behind your friend Brian's house after drinking too much Peach Schnapps you recognized that something was missing. Where was the warmth? The safety and comfort? The milk?

That brand of question haunts Lactaphiliacs, i.e. those harboring a sexual attraction to lactating breasts: "Where's the milk? Will you show me the milk? Will you squirt the milk all over my face? Will you allow some guy to take pictures of you being milked by another woman and then publish them on the Internet for my gratification?"

PSYCHOLOGICAL ORIGINS

For the Lactaphiliac, somewhere along the line the healthy relationship with breast milk morphs into an obsessive one, and a function of human anatomy that typically grows less interesting to people as they mature instead becomes a source of erotic fascination. (It's one thing to admire a woman's breasts, but quite another to fantasize about getting nourishment from them. After the age of, say, two. Or fifteen, anyway.) As with so many fetishes, Lactaphilia likely springs from a traumatic or over-stimulating childhood experience in which breastfeeding and excitement are forever linked in the mind.

Despite being rather mammocentric, Lactaphilia is not solely a pleasure for men. The milk of human kindness comes served in a nice tall glass. For some women, breastfeeding their children may stir up certain sexual energies. Some have even been known to achieve orgasm during feeding.

CONSIDERATIONS

If you're into it, go for it. There's not really anything dangerous going on here, unless you're afraid of getting squirted in the eye.

Of Note . . .

Although many people don't realize it, men in fact do possess mammary glands and are capable of lactating. With hormonal stimulus—often caused by treatments given to combat prostate cancer—men may find themselves squirting milk. Lactation may also occur in men through massage of the mammary tissue or consistent suckling at the nipple over a period of months.

NASOPHILIA
(ALSO RHINOPHILIA)

The sexual attraction to the rose smeller.

USEFUL ACCOUTREMENTS

○ face

○ nose

THE FANTASY

Your friends say you're better off without him, and maybe they're right. He could be selfish and cold. But your friends will never understand what he did have, something that stood out as so beautiful among all of his faults.

At night, you would lie in bed beside him, listening to that glorious sucking sound. The air went in, the air went out, and your very heartbeat slowed to its steady rhythm. In profile, set against the bedroom window, his nose was limned by

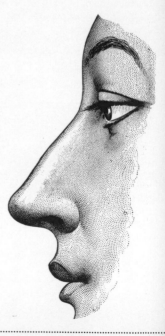

angelic moonlight, and, as he slept, you would trace the large angles of that gigantic proboscis.

If there were only a way that you could leave him, but keep that fantastic nose, what a happy life the two of you could lead. Curling up in the garden beside the nose, smelling the fragrant aromas of the flowerbed. You would care for it. Keep it clean. Blow it when necessary. If only . . .

WHAT IS IT?

The human nose may come in a variety of shapes and sizes, depending upon the ethmoid bone and nasal septum contained therein. They range from dainty-and-petite to *give-me-back-my-oxygen!*-large. They may be straight, sloped, thick, thin, bulbous, snub or turned-up. And for every single type, there's a person out there who wants to rub his or her genitals all over it. Thank God for Nasophilia!

Just as there are many types of noses, there are many things that people want to do with other people's noses. While one man might be happy to sit in a coffee shop and simply admire the beautifully huge hawk-like beak of the young barista, another man across town may be euphorically licking the curves and crevices of his wife's wide-nostrilled face. And elsewhere in town, a woman is chatting up a smart fellow with a long, lean proboscis, considering the multitude of places he might be enticed to stick it.

In *Psychopathia Sexualis*, Austrian psychiatrist Richard Freiherr von Krafft-Ebing told the story of a man who fantasized about meeting a woman with a nose so large that he could penetrate it with his member. As luck would have it, he eventually found one such woman and immediately proposed marriage. As bad luck would have it, she declined and eventually had him arrested for stalking her.

PSYCHOLOGICAL ORIGINS

It's not difficult to speculate on why a person might see the nose as an erogenous protrusion. After all, it is smack dab in the middle of the face and goes a great way toward defining the way a person looks. Traditionally, very large noses have been considered ugly or shameful, and this may explain why some people fetishize the big ones, as a way of feeling superiority over a sexual partner or of enjoying that which is socially illicit.

CONSIDERATIONS

Generally speaking, Nasophilia is a relatively harmless fetish. If an appreciation for and attraction to an unconventional nose can help two people find one another, then that's pretty okay. However, if your fetish grows to the point where you're chasing imaginary Pinocchios, you may find yourself rather lonely.

Some people enjoy substituting noses for penises in intercourse, sometimes intentionally sneezing or blowing to simulate orgasm. This is an excellent way of contracting or passing along illnesses.

Of Note...

In his novel *Wake Up, Sir!*, Jonathan Ames has his narrator experience a *"coup de foudre par le nez"* when he meets a beautiful woman and falls in love with her particularly oddly shaped nose. "A nose! The most incredible nose I had ever seen in my life. Enormous, bumpy, hooked, with flaring nostrils the size of shot glasses. The nose looked like some sort of mad knot on a tree . . . " The narrator fantasizes about kissing and caressing the woman's nose and muses that he has perhaps invented a never-before-seen fetish. (Clearly, not the case.)

NECROPHILIA
(ALSO NECROLAGNIA, THANATOPHILIA)

The predilection for la grand morte.

USEFUL ACCOUTREMENTS

- ○ hearse
- ○ keys to mortuary
- ○ darkness
- ○ shovel

THE FANTASY

It's been nineteen months since you last saw her. How does the time slip past so furtively, like a grave robber in the night? It was after dinner in the parking lot that she asked you. You wanted to say yes—you tried—but you weren't able. And that was the last time you saw her . . . until now. Until you walked into this room and saw her through the cheerless crowd. She looks the same, really. Her hair is slightly longer, her skin a tad more sallow, but she's clearly still the same woman whose heart you broke.

Or is she? You cross the floor to where she's resting and feel something bubble in your chest. There's something different about her. A—a what?—an *energy* she radiates now. This is new. This is something very new. You find your hand reaching toward her hand. Your lips pursing for her mouth. Her lips are cold against your tongue. Your face is flushed. This is something powerful. This is love. *This* was what she wanted all that time ago! And only now are you able to give it. You look down upon her lovely, unmoving face, and you've never wanted anyone, anything, more. It's amazing what a fatal aneurysm can do to some people.

Maybe she'll have some time to get reacquainted between the viewing and the interment.

WHAT IS IT?

So, you wanna have sex with a dead person. And why not? Dead people are so much less combative than their non-dead counterparts. They never ask for the remote. They never go rambling on long, tedious stories about some guy at the office who has a daughter who does something or other with homeless alpacas. It's just blissful quiet. Sure, they may smell a little weird, but you get used to that.

Welcome to a tradition that goes all the way back to when people first started dying. Did you think you were the first person ever to want to fornicate with a member of the recently (or not so recently) deceased? Heavens no! The Greek historian Herodotus wrote of the practice occurring way back in ancient Egypt. And don't think you're the only one doing it today. Many people in the know, including unabashed necrophile Karen Greenlee, stress that it goes on a lot more than you might think. Exactly how often is unknown. Necrophiliacs are secretive, and it's even harder to get information from dead people.

Perhaps you're not ready to jump with both feet into a sensual grave. You can still enjoy the exanimate thrill of Necrophilia with a little role-playing. All you have to do is convince your partner that there's nothing creepy about one of you pretending to be lain out on the mortuary slab while the other gets to work. Simple!

PSYCHOLOGICAL ORIGINS

There are many reasons a person might turn to Necrophilia. You may suffer from such low self-esteem that you believe the only obtainable partner is the one who physically can't say no. You may have a serious fear of death, and this is your way of gaining control over it. It may be that a phobia of dead bodies has manifested itself in you as a sexual attraction to them. Or maybe you just dig rot.

CONSIDERATIONS

Necrophilia is considered a felony in at least four U.S. states and a misdemeanor in at least five others. There is currently no federal legislature against the practice itself, though laws about handling a corpse, raiding a cemetery, and failing to report a death, for example, do apply. Before deciding to engage in Necrophiliac activity, you may want to inquire about its legality in your state of residence. Knowing is half of having sexual intercourse with the physical remains of a human being.

Of Note . . .

Although a complete poll of practicing Necrophiliacs has not been achieved, it is believed that nine-tenths are men and two-thirds are big Marilyn Manson fans.

PODOPHILIA (ALSO ARETIFISM)

The fascination with feet.

USEFUL ACCOUTREMENTS

- O   the one that went to market
- O   the one that stayed home
- O   the one that had roast beef
- O   the one that had none
- O   the one that went *wee wee wee* all the way home

THE FANTASY

Just keep looking. Eventually, you're going to find the job that's right for you. The job that perfectly matches your interests and know-how. Who cares if you've been through the employment section of this paper every day now for the past six years? Any day now, that magical opportunity is going to appear. There's only one thing in the world that you really care about, and you just cannot give up on the dream.

Wait, look! There, below the ad for filing clerk! Could it be? The position you've so long dreamed of? "Help wanted: *Foot Deodorant Test Sniffer*." That's it! The dream job!

Just pray you ace the interview.

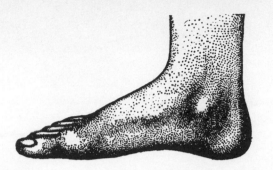

WHAT IS IT?

Whereas modern fetishism has really only hit its stride in the past two hundred or so years—i.e. The Golden Age of Perversion—people have had an appreciation for the foot throughout history, and not necessarily sexually. It has been written about, sketched, painted, and lovingly crafted in sculpture. This appreciation makes sense; the foot is what allows humans to walk upright, unlike other animals. For millions of years, it was pretty much the only way for people to get around. Obviously, it deserved to be thought of highly.

About a thousand years ago, "foot love" got a little twisted with the introduction of foot binding. Small and dainty feet have always been favored over big clunky ones, so eventually the Chinese adopted the practice of wrapping little girls' feet to keep them small and dainty forever, and thus beautiful (provided nobody ever had to look at the unbound foot).

Foot fetishism today is much less painful and deformity-inducing. Compared to binding, toe-sucking and sole-licking seem genuinely romantic. And there are so many fun things you can do with a foot. Like jumping is pretty fun, for instance. Or toe-pointing. Or a whole bunch of other, weirder stuff that we won't get into here.

PSYCHOLOGICAL ORIGINS

Like so many other fetishes, this one likely spawns in childhood. As a toddler, you constantly engaged with your parents eye-to-foot. Maybe your mother pushed you around the kitchen floor with her feet to keep you occupied while she talked on the phone. Maybe your father let you grab onto his big toe while he sat watching television. Feet had good connotations. Maybe your incredibly pretty aunt with the huge breasts who never wears a t-shirt loose enough to adequately cover them used to lean over your crib and grab your foot and make that *brrrrrrrr* sound on the sensitive sole of your foot.

The biggest problem facing Podophiles today is shame. You may not want to out yourself as a foot fetishist because they tend to get teased in society, even though nearly one in every one hundred adult men are full-on Podophiles. And certainly a lot more than that really enjoy the foot. But if you harbor unhappy feelings toward your predilection, it could have a negative effect on your sexual life. And if you bottle all that up, it might come out in weird ways. Wouldn't you rather be known as the guy who likes feet than the guy who was arrested for licking random women's toes at the movie theater?

BODIES, PARTS & FUNCTIONS

Of Note . . .

The word "foot" or "feet" appears in the King James Bible well over 400 times, including this quote from Isaiah 49:23: " . . . they shall bow down to thee with their face toward the earth, and lick up the dust of thy feet." While that's taken somewhat out of context, it's still not incredibly unlike what you might read on any of the bazillion-and-three foot fetish sites on the Internet.

The word "elbow" appears in the King James Bible once.

TRICHOPHILIA

The love of locks for which there are no key.

○   five million hair follicles   ○   conditioner

THE FANTASY

These are the sensations you've been dreaming of for so long: the sandpapery drag across your cheek, the thousand sharp bristles of this beard piercing your chin as the two of you lie locked in romantic embrace. . . . Who would've ever guessed that something so unpleasant—something so *painful*—would linger for all those lonely months in which the two of you were separated? It's the least expected lure that draws the lover in.

And now that you've been reunited, will you tell? Is it too shameful to reveal that through all those cold, dark nights, you remained not only faithful, but unable? That there was no other who could provide this feeling for you, and that you instead chose to sleep alone? That the closest you could come to infidelity was with a hairbrush? But even scraping that across your face left you feeling hollow and forlorn.

Should you tell? Or does your lover already know? Does she realize that she provides something so special? You have to tell her.

After all, the bearded lady only comes to town so often.

WHAT IS IT?

Long, cascading blond hair. Short, pixie-cut dark hair. A shock of brilliant red hair. Glorious flowing mullets. Mustachios. Muttonchops. Beards. Back hair. Shoulder hair. Arm hair. Leg hair. Chest hair. Nipple hair. Pubic hair.

Does any of that do it for you? Don't be embarrassed. If you spend your nights beneath the bed sheets caressing a string-tied lock of your junior-high crush's ponytail, step forward. If you need to twist your little finger inside a lock of your lover's mane in order to climax, come clean. If you can imagine no greater sensation than the texture of fuzzy armpit against your tongue, stand tall! You're not alone. You're certainly not the first Trichophiliac, nor will you be the last.

Trichophilia, in case you haven't been tipped off by this point, is the fetishizing of hair—hair of all textures, colors, and types. As a fetish, this makes a certain amount of sense; the human body is almost completely covered with hair follicles. Ironically, the sex organs are some of the very few parts of the body that *aren't* fuzzy, but this deficiency is most likely why some of the body's thickest hair grows just beside the genitals: for protection. And possibly adornment.

But take note: There is a difference between being attracted to a certain type of hair and actually having a hair fetish. You may enjoy gazing down at the back of a strawberry-blond head while working your love magic, but that's not quite the same thing as keeping an array of wigs in your closet for any potential bedroom guests because you need them to get off. (The wigs, not the guests.)

PSYCHOLOGICAL ORIGINS

Hair has been an attractive accessory for people since before they were people. If you were a dashing young *Australopithecus africanus* man cruising through the savannas of Ethiopia three million years ago, and you saw two pretty little hominids—one smooth and the other hairy—you would have a choice to make. The hairless one may look better in a bikini someday when bikinis are invented, but that would be pretty far from your mind. You'd want to make certain your kids live long enough to grow into strong *Homo rudolfensises*, and since they'll be spending less and less time in the forests, they're going to need all the hair they can get to protect them from the harmful rays of the sun. So you'd grab the hairy one by a thick tuft and force her into a beautiful act of love.

Granted, things have changed considerably in the past several million years, but a nice head of hair is still looked upon as a sign of virility. Humans are instinctively attracted to hair. Attraction to a certain type of hair may become a fetish if it is tied to particular arousing, comforting, or frightening childhood memories. For example, if a child were molested by an *Australopithecus africanus* with a handlebar moustache, that person might grow up to be attracted only to *Australopithecus africanuses* with handlebar moustaches.

CONSIDERATIONS

Be wary of taking your Trichophilia too far. You can read "too far" as meaning "to jail." In 2002, Michael Howard, a.k.a. the Hair Bandit of California, was arrested for grabbing ten separate women and cutting the hair from their head with scissors or a knife. He was convicted and sentenced to eight years in prison. If you really need hair that bad, please consider buying a wig.

UROPHILIA
(ALSO UROLAGNIA, UNDINISM)

The quest for the Golden Shower.

USEFUL ACCOUTREMENTS

- ○ water
- ○ coffee
- ○ tea
- ○ beer
- ○ hydrochlorothiazide

THE FANTASY

He's so beautiful. Look at him. Everything about him exudes sexuality. The way he brushes his hair back. The way he holds his water glass so firmly in his hand. The way he twists his lips around the mouth of a beer bottle. And here you are alone in his living room. This is the time. You have to tell him what you want. You have to tell him what you want him to do to you. You have to tell him now. Do it. Do it now!

"There's something I need to tell you," you say nervously.

"Hold that thought," he says, standing up and walking toward the bathroom. "I'm gonna go use the john."

No! your heart cries out. *Wait! Wait for just one—*

"Unless," he says, "maybe you'd like to come in there with me?"

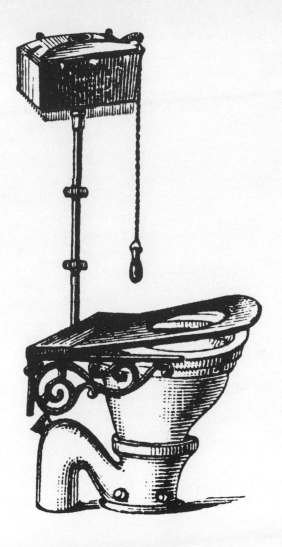

UROPHILIA

WHAT IS IT?

If one of your coworkers were to walk up to your desk, hand you a folder full of expense reports, and then just literally pee all over you, you'd most likely be somewhat upset, more than a little disgusted, and quite a bit wetter than you'd prefer. Why in the world, then, would you let—or maybe even *want*—someone to pee on you in the bedroom? Doesn't make sense, does it? Well, how about if that same obnoxious coworker (and, really, why hasn't he been fired?) were to spit in your mouth while you were yawning? How would you feel then? Upset? Disgusted? Violent? But would that stop you from letting the cute intern who still hasn't figured out how to use the color copier stick his tongue down your throat? The point is, when it comes to bodily fluids, it's all about context.

For the discerning Urophiliac, there is nothing sexier than a warm stream pouring forth from the one he or she loves (or lusts). And there are many ways to play water sports. In fact, you can use pee for pretty much anything. All it takes is a little imagination, and some pee.

Urophilia is often incorporated into BDSM play, with the dominant urinating on the submissive as a form of humiliation. But for a lot of Urophiliacs, there's nothing humiliating about it at all. It's just another way to say "I love you." Or at least, "I like you enough to pee on you."

When it comes to bodily fluids, it's all about context.

PSYCHOLOGICAL ORIGINS

For many Urophiliacs, it's the stigma attached to urine that makes water sports so erotic. It may be that they enjoy feeling like they're doing something dirty. Or it may be a way to show a complete acceptance of or infatuation for their partner. Plus it comes off as pretty hardcore.

CONSIDERATIONS

Despite the fact that urinating is an excretory function of the body, if you and your partner are both healthy and disease free, Urophilia is relatively harmless, even if you're planning to ingest. (Of course, *not* peeing on people is also safe and harmless.)

INANIMATE OBJECTS

AUTOMOTIVE FETISH

The desire for a hot fuel injection.

USEFUL ACCOUTREMENTS

- car
- garage
- privacy
- Sammy Hagar CD

THE FANTASY

Ah, this is the best. There's truly no better way to spend a Saturday night than working on your car. Sure, some of your buddies might enjoy taking their girlfriends out to dinner or a strip club or whatever, but when it comes down to it you'd rather be in the garage burning up some real, honest-to-goodness elbow grease.

Besides, cars get dirty. They have to be cleaned often. And you take cleaning your car seriously—no buff rags for you, ho no, just your chest. Your bare chest. Maybe it's a little weird, but can you think of a better way to rub hot oil all over a car's hood? A car's sleek, beautiful, gently undulating hood? In slow, circular motions, up and down and around and around . . .

And when the wax runs out, you always know just the right tool for cleaning out the inside of the exhaust pipe.

WHAT IS IT?

People love sex. People love their cars. People love having sex in their cars. The question is, why has it only
recently come to light that people might enjoy having
sex *with* their cars? In actuality, people have probably
been tonguing chrome bumpers and humping bucket
seats for a while now. (A good rule of thumb is: If you
can imagine it, somebody's almost certainly doing it.)
But the Automotive Fetish only really hit the big-time
in early 2007 when Chris Donald, a British mechanic,
came out to a newspaper and subsequently published
the very helpful document "How to Make Love to a
Car or Other Vehicle" on the Internet, based on his
own experience and that of other Automotive Fetishists
he's encountered.

   In the document, the auto-amorous mechanic gives
interested readers heaps of useful advice ("The tailpipe
isn't the only option!") and safety tips ("Most fluids would
be hazardous if swallowed"), but what it really comes

down to is this: The fetish does not come standard; you'll need to customize it to suit your desires. You can drape yourself across your car's hood, give its shocks a good test, snuggle up to the interior, or crawl underneath and enjoy the view. Whatever honks your horn.

And you need not limit yourself to the four-wheeled variety. Most vehicles aren't, by nature, monogamous, so there's no reason for you to be. Go see a drive-in movie with a motorcycle. Take a romantic sunset cruise with a speed-boat. And, if you like to play on the edge, meet a hulking eighteen-wheeler at a highway rest stop for a secretive and passionate tête-à-tête. (Just make sure you get permission from the vehicles' owners before doing anything risqué. Most people still have rather puritanical belief systems regarding their vehicles.)

PSYCHOLOGICAL ORIGINS

The Automotive Fetish is so rare and newly acknowledged that it has received little, if any, serious psychological study. However, it does share many similarities with the Robofetish (page 188), so this may be seen as another step toward an increasingly object-oriented view of sexuality. On one hand, the Automotive Fetish pushes the Robofetish to the point of sexualizing objects that don't even resemble humans. On the other hand, people love their cars, and they do tend to be somewhat animistic with them, anthropomorphizing and assigning personalities to them. Just look at *Knight Rider*, *The Love Bug*, and *Transformers* if you need proof.

Aside from that, cars are often seen as masculine symbols. Powerful, well-tuned, fast. Many men go to great lengths to make certain their cars are always in excellent condition, internally and externally. It's certainly not a coincidence that automotive magazines and garbagey hair band music videos are filled with images of half-naked women straddling the hoods of souped-up sports cars.

CONSIDERATIONS

The term "safe sex" takes on a slightly different meaning in regard to automotive love. While you're unlikely to contract a disease or become pregnant with little baby Matchbox cars after a romantic tryst, you may very well, if you're not careful, come down with a severe case of singed flesh or smashed-to-death-beneath-a-two-ton-piece-of-machinery-itis. Just be smart about what you do and how you're doing it.

BALLOON FETISH
(ALSO BALLOONISM, INFLATABLE FETISH)

The dalliance that goes pop.

USEFUL ACCOUTREMENTS

- red balloons
- blue balloons
- yellow balloons
- green balloons
- air
- a mouth

THE FANTASY

A scene like this should be illegal. There's no way that they should let a woman do this sort of thing in a public park. In front of a line of children, no less! All standing there, waiting for the nice lady to blow them up one of their own. For her dainty yet practiced hands to twist, squeeze, and stuff those  beautiful things into a menagerie of shapes. That sound, the chirping of rubber against rubber . . . ooh, it's going to drive you insane.

She's reaching into her bag for yet another one. This could go on all day! Licking her lips before pressing them against the flaccid material. Look at her chest expand as she expels her sweet breath and awakens another delightful little figure. Does she notice you watching? Is there a part of her that knows what she's doing to you? She's still blowing. It's getting pretty full. She's *still* blowing. She has to stop. It's going to— It's going to—

Pop!

Oh dear. You need to get to a bathroom, quick.

WHAT IS IT?

Balloon Fetishists make up one of the fastest growing fetish communities. While just a few years ago you would have had no safe place to discuss your penchant for transforming harmless rubber sacs into faux-bodily orifices, the Internet has changed all that. Now you can do a quick online search and lose yourself in website after infantilizing website.

Looners (as they call themselves) can generally be divided into two categories, regardless of whether they prefer their balloon play with a partner or alone: poppers and non-poppers. The non-poppers form a sort of emotional connection to their balloons. They derive pleasure from blowing them up to their full potential, savoring the squeaky sound of stretching membrane and the sensation of taut latex against their skin. Once they've had their fun, they'll usually untie the balloon to release the air and put it away for safekeeping. Poppers, on the other hand, enjoy the potential and kinetic energy a balloon represents. They sense erotic tension in the uncertain waiting, raw sexuality in the explosion. They'll sometimes pop several balloons at a go, either with a pin or beneath their body weight. The two groups often have very different philosophies toward balloons, a source of contention within the looner community. The non-poppers feel the poppers are being disrespectful to the balloons, while the poppers look at the non-poppers like, "Um, it's a *balloon*."

PSYCHOLOGICAL ORIGINS

Unsurprisingly, most Balloon Fetishes have their seeds in childhood memories, often traumatic ones. Children may develop love/fear relationships with balloons. On one hand, they're playthings, often given out at parties. They're pretty, and fun, and somewhat magical. On the other hand, they can pop loudly and unexpectedly. Either (and oftentimes both) of these strong emotional responses may lead to sexual feelings as a person grows into adolescence.

One thing that many balloon fetishists have remarked upon is the scent. There are few things in the world that smell like a balloon. And because the olfactory sense is closely related to memory, that powdery-sour chemical smell is likely to send just about any adult crashing back toward his or her childhood. And, for many looners, those childhood memories are at precisely the core of their sexual fascination.

CONSIDERATIONS

For God's sake, be smart about how you choose a balloon to bring home to your bedroom. Balloons found at party supply shops and toy stores can usually be counted on to be safe. But the balloons you find soliciting themselves on street corners, beneath underpasses, or in the back pages of weekly alternative papers may be carrying diseases. It's a good idea to use a condom when engaging in sexual relations with an unknown balloon.

INANIMATE OBJECTS

Of Note . . .

The Balloon Fetish may be closely related to a number of other fetishes. Many looners, for example, enjoy watching women pop balloons beneath their bare feet or in high heels (see Podophilia, 68; Retifism, 98; Crush Fetish, 130). However, one fetish to which it is almost never related is Pedophilia, a distinction looners will go to great lengths to make clear.

HIEROPHILIA
(ALSO THEOPHILIA)

The desire to be sinful with unsinful things.

USEFUL ACCOUTREMENTS

- psalm book
- rosary beads
- altar
- cross
- highly forgiving Holy Father

THE FANTASY

Your mother's mad at you again. Why must you break the rules? Why must you ignore curfew? Why can't you be more like your older sister? She's practically a nun, home by seven every night and saying her prayers before bed by nine. You are a disappointment to the family.

What you need is penance. So your mother goes into the cabinet and returns to your room with a small porcelain statuette of St. Gerard, the patron saint of children and good confessions. What she doesn't know is how familiar with it you already are, having snuck into the cabinet so many times to stroke the figure's smooth curves. Now, reunited, you run your pinky finger along the well-known grooves of the saint's face. Your mouth goes dry at the touch.

You are to stay alone in your room with the statuette, your mother says, and think about what you've done. Just you and the statue. "Certainly, Mother. Whatever you wish."

WHAT IS IT?

One would think that Hierophilia, or a sexual attraction to holy objects or places, would by definition be motivated by an urge toward blasphemy, toward desecrating power-ful religious idolatry. In fact, the opposite is true; most Hierophiliacs are actually quite devoted.

If you're a religious person who is alive today in the Western world, it may be hard for you to imagine the urge to fantasize about all the things a creative person could do with a set of rosary beads. Or to dream of screaming "Oh, God!" on an actual altar of worship. Then again, it may not. If you were raised to believe that these things were imbued with an unearthly significance, might they not stimulate the same trigger in your psyche that nudges you toward going forth and multiplying?

PSYCHOLOGICAL ORIGINS

A crossroads between religion and sex seems, in a way, inevitable. Over here, you have consecrated ground and a bunch of holy objects you've been taught to believe are filled with immaculate energy and power. And over here, you have a physical attraction to objects and ideas that arouse strong emotions. The two are bound to meet at some point.

A crossroads between religion and sex seems, in a way, inevitable.

CONSIDERATIONS

If you're a religious person, you should tread carefully into any Hierophilic activities. Although it may be gratifying at the time, it may very well stir up feelings of guilt that can be damaging both spiritually and sexually. If you're not a religious person, have at it. What's it to you?

Of Note . . .

Many religions throughout time did not share Jewish, Christian, and Muslim views about sex, and included fertility goddesses in their coterie of divine beings. Some even encouraged sexual practices as religious rites. The Chandela temples of Khajuraho, India—built in the Tenth Century—are covered with sculptures of people engaged in acts that would make many people blush today.

PLUSHOPHILIA
(ALSO PEDIOPHILIA)

The preference for soft and cuddly sex toys.

USEFUL ACCOUTREMENTS

- cloth
- thread
- cotton stuffing
- miniature butt plug

THE FANTASY

Oh, Mr. Boffo! That feels so nice. Your fuzzy bottom is so smooth. And soft. And sexy. You make me feel alive. What's that, Mr. Boffo? You want me to do *what*? Put it *where*? Are you sure? Mr. Boffo, you've just made me the hip-hip-happiest person in the whole wide world. Oh, Mr. Boffo. Mr. Boffo. Mr. Boffo! Mr. Boffooooooooooooo!!!

No matter what happens in this callous and cruel world, you can sleep comfortably in the knowledge that your faithful Woofward and Grrrstein will always be there for you, lying snuggly beneath your arm. What would you do without those two cuddly stuffed dogs that wait dutifully on your unmade bed for when you need them most? You can always count on their cheerful faces—felt tongues dangling so adorably from their ever-present smiles—to pick you up when you're feeling down in the frown. They truly are your best friends. So much more reliable than all the people you know.

But let's say you long for a way to take that snuggly relationship to the next level. Let's say you've sketched out a whole scenario and know, in detail, how you'd like to advance things with your fuzzy friends. Let's say you've actually *enacted* said scenario. Then you, sir, are in all probability a Plushophile.

Plushophiles find pleasure in stuffed animals above and beyond what the average toddler or Beanie Baby collector might. Never mind that this sometimes involves a little at-home surgery—undoing a few stitches in the seam along Woofward's legs, for example, or poking a hole in the back of Grrrstein's cute little mouth. The great thing about Plushophilia is, whatever you're in the mood for, you can feel confident you've found consenting partners.

INANIMATE OBJECTS

PSYCHOLOGICAL ORIGINS

You probably know at least one person who has an inordinate number of stuffed animals on his or her bed. That doesn't mean that he or she has sex with one or all of those stuffed animals. In many cases, it may be due to a desire to hold on to some comforting aspect of childhood innocence. Collecting plush toys is an extremely popular hobby, even among adults. In fact, there are conventions regularly held around the countries so that "plushies" can meet up, talk plush, and buy more stuffed animals. Only a small percentage of plushies are Plushophiliacs. (And the word "Plushophilia," confusingly, is sometimes used in a non-sexual way to mean "plush toy enthusiasts.")

Why some small percentage of plushies develops sexual attractions to the toys is open to a toy store full of speculation. There hasn't been a great deal of research into the matter, probably because no one's getting hurt. But, for the sexually active plushies, those conventions are terrific places to meet human partners who share their interests. And some of them find some pretty interesting ways to have fun together. (See Fursuit Fetish, page 168.)

Plush toys almost never carry any contractible diseases, so the sex is always safe. And, because they're so amazingly accommodating to your needs, desires, and appetites, you don't even have to worry about hurting the little guy's feelings. No safe words necessary.

Your biggest problem will be cleanup. What some Plushophiles suggest is buying two of the same plush toy: one for safekeeping and the other for play. If that's not an option for whatever reason, you can wash yours. Bubble Gund, a product sold specifically for cleaning plush toys, comes highly recommended on several plushie websites.

INANIMATE OBJECTS

Of Note . . .

If Plushophilia Internet message boards are to be believed, the stuffed Meeko doll, based on the oh-so-cute raccoon character from Disney's *Pocahontas*, seems to be the Brad Pitt of plush toys. Wanna know why? Sorry. Meeko doesn't kiss and tell.

RETIFISM

The understanding that you can't love a person until you've walked a mile while sniffing her shoes.

USEFUL ACCOUTREMENTS

- O flats
- O high heels
- O stiletto heels
- O killer heels
- O boots

- O sneakers
- O clogs
- O loafers
- O moccasins
- O espadrilles

THE FANTASY

Oh, gosh! Is it seven o'clock already? How does the night pass so quickly? Looks like it's going to be another cold, wet day. You can hear the sleet hitting the windowpanes from here. Don't get out of bed. Call in sick. You're not going to survive another day at the office.

And how can you leave such a beautiful and sexy thing behind in this warm bed? Just stay here; stay here and snuggle. Wrap your arms around her and hold her close to your chest. Maybe the rest of the world will just vanish. Dissipate into nothingness, and there'll be nothing left except for this bed. And you. And the love of your life . . .

this gray suede high-heeled boot that has brought you so much happiness.

Oh, gray suede high-heeled boot, you must have fallen from the feet of an angel!

WHAT IS IT?

The are two kinds of shoe fetishism. One is "Oh my God, that shoe is so cute; I need to buy it!" and the other is "Oh my God, that shoe is so sexy; I want to run my tongue along its corrugated muddy sole." One is held mainly by women, and the other mainly by men. One is embodied by Imelda Marcos, the former first lady of the Philippines, and the second by Nicolas-Edme Rétif de la Bretonne, eponymic 18th-century French novelist and rival of the Marquis de Sade. This chapter will be dealing with the latter.

While Retifism is related to Podophilia (page 68), it is not necessarily the same thing. Don't jump to conclusions; fetishists are more clever than that, and many draw very harsh lines. Retifism is an attraction to the *shoe*, not the foot. Sure, there might be a foot in the shoe. Pish posh. That's neither here nor there. The shoe is the thing. Retifists love shoes. They can't get enough of them. They ogle them. They buy them. They collect them. They steal them. They caress them and tongue them and sniff them and rub them all over their Retifist selves.

If you're a Retifist, there are probably a few factors that really do it for you. The way a shoe looks, so petite and elegant. The way it feels, so soft and sleek. And, most importantly, the way it smells. Maybe you're a new-shoe man, and you get off on that cured leather smell. Or perhaps you like yours used. The things a woman's sweaty, callused foot will do to a shoe's bouquet . . . Sigh!

A Retifist may not be content to simply fondle and inhale shoes. Some actually prefer to destroy the shoe by ripping it to shreds in a fit of ecstasy.

PSYCHOLOGICAL ORIGINS

Like Podophilia, the origins of your Retifism can probably be traced back to childhood. Most likely, you were crawling across the floor toward your mother when you were struck by her smart pair of leather-trimmed Gucci mules. That revelation, coupled with your inability to connect with women as equals, sealed the deal.

If you're going to start building your own collection of women's shoes, it is highly recommended that you *buy* them. While a number of Retifists swear by the excitement of stealing the objects of their desire—some even going so far as to pull them off of women's feet before hauling ass out of the park—this is almost certainly a bad idea. If caught, not only will you be labeled a thief, but also a pervert, and an inconsiderate one at that. Nothing will damage your reputation faster than a photo of you being tackled by a police officer while you've got a sandal dangling from your teeth.

Of Note . . .

Altocalciphilia, the attraction to high-heeled shoes specifically, is probably the largest subset of Retifism. In fact, high heels became prominent footwear in the United States only after they'd already proven to be extremely popular amongst patrons in brothels. Richard von Krafft-Ebing hypothesized that most Retifists are also masochists, and this can be seen most acutely in Altocalciphilia, where the long and sharp heels are often used to inflict pain upon submissive men—most popularly in the genitals.

SITOPHILIA

The gastronomy of sex.

USEFUL ACCOUTREMENTS

- 3 eggs
- ¼ cup vegetable oil
- ¾ cup sugar
- 2 cups all-purpose flour
- 1 tsp. baking soda
- 1 tsp. baking powder
- ½ tsp. ground cinnamon
- salt, to taste

THE FANTASY

You've just spent hours bent over the stove. The sink is piled high with encrusted utensils and saucepans. The atmosphere of the kitchen is an ingredient-infused fog. Your skin, clothes, and hair are covered in layers of grease. But finally, your work is complete and you lay out a serving tray before your husband: canard en croûte de lavande. He eyes the glistening bird hungrily, his mouth wet with anticipation, and reaches for a knife and fork.

A knife and fork? He wants to eat it? What the hell?! You didn't spend the entire afternoon chopping shallots and glazing duck just so that he can spend ten minutes shoving it down his throat. Does he have no desire to rip off a tender leg and slip it down your panties? Or grab onto your hair and shove your face into the sticky sweet mess? Or mash a handful of potato between his palms and rub them up and down your thighs before scraping it off with his teeth?

What is it with men? They just don't get it.

Humans' desires for food and sex have always been somewhat intertwined. The Homo ergaster who could bring his woman a dead rabbit to gnaw on was more likely to enjoy a roll in the dirt than the one who couldn't. Today, the Homo sapiens may not have to hunt for rabbit, but buying his lady one at a fancy restaurant can have similar rewards.

At some point, the eating and the sex merged, as somebody got an idea and said to his or her partner: "Hey, let's not just eat this food. Let's roll around in it, smear it all over each other's bodies, and then eat it off of each other while grinding on the dining room floor." That was the birth of Sitophilia, the use of food as a sexual toy. Before you knew it, people were filling bathtubs with cottage cheese, selling ranch-flavored edible underwear, and emptying the contents of refrigerators onto Kim Basinger. Whipped cream profits went through the roof.

Sitophilia, more than practically any other fetish, is all things to all people. Its possibilities are endless. If you and your partner can open up a bag of pretzels with a creative mind, you can be a Sitophiliac.

Food can be used during sex in so many ways that it's nearly impossible to generalize a particular brand of Sitophilia's origins. But by examining how you use the food, you may be able to draw your own conclusions. If you enjoy being tied to the bedposts while your partner drips hot pork fat onto your genitals, that's almost certainly a form of BDSM play. If you need the smell of curry to get excited, then perhaps your first sexual experience occurred in an Indian restaurant. If you and your partner enjoy licking whipped cream off each other's chests, more likely than not, one of you has been reading a women's magazine recently. If you hide freshly baked mince pies on ladies' chairs just to watch them accidentally sit on them and then you go home and masturbate to the memory, then maybe, jeez, you should go talk to a psychologist.

INANIMATE OBJECTS

Before you knew it, people were filling bathtubs with cottage cheese.

CONSIDERATIONS

Food sex is really no different from any other kind of sex. The most important things to remember are to be smart and be kind. Limits for pain, discomfort, humiliation, stickiness, and fat content should all be decided beforehand.

Also, remember that most foods rot very quickly, particularly so when they're shoved inside a bodily orifice. Make certain to clean yourself thoroughly, inside and out, after any Sitophilia play.

Limits for pain, discomfort, humiliation, stickiness, and fat content should all be decided beforehand.

Of Note . . .

Two thousand years ago, some of the more excitable citizens of Rome used to partake in huge orgies, melding food and sex in celebration of Bacchus, the god of wine. Revelers would gorge themselves on food, drink themselves stupid, and then have as much sex with as many people as they could manage before passing out in a blithering heap.

Contrary to popular belief, these were not common activities of the general citizenry. In fact, they were, for the most part, illegal. The government believed that dangerous alliances and collectives could be formed within their shadowy recesses. (Wouldn't that just be your luck? To go to an orgy and get stuck next to the guy who won't stop talking politics?)

FANTASYLAND

INFLATION FETISH

The desire to get blown . . . up.

USEFUL ACCOUTREMENTS

- latex suit
- rubber hose
- air pump
- healthy imagination

THE FANTASY

Her long, nimble fingers dancing along the stem of her wine glass, her eyes boring smugly into your own, she is so confident, so aloof. She has no idea what strange fate awaits her. And she holds its seed right there in her hand.

Lifting the glass from the table, she floats it in small circles before her eyes and then watches the dark liquor swirl slowly back into an unmoving plane, glowing in the sunlight of the outdoor café. "I'm so happy to hear that we can let bygones be bygones," she says, bringing the crystal rim to her perfect scarlet lips.

"Of course," you say. "I'm happy just to keep you in my life. If only as a friend." She does not sip. Why won't she sip? Does she know?

"I knew you'd feel that way," she says. "You were always so . . . nice." She sips.

The transformation begins instantly. First with her lips, which grow to the size of two red baseballs. And then her breasts. You can hear the hiss of air filling them as they overtake her chest, stretching her blouse to the limits of its stitching. The look on her face is priceless. Soon, her entire body is round and taut, like a beautiful woman-sized volleyball. Will she be happy to see you gone from her life now? How soon until she takes you back? How soon until she's begging you to take her back?

And then she begins to rise. The hissing does not subside. She continues to expand. She's the size of a small car now, but lighter than air. Her chair tips over as she takes to the sky. You jump up to grab her foot, but all you come back with is one delicate sandal. She's above the buildings, in the clouds, a speck in the sky. Maybe you gave her too much elixir.

WHAT IS IT?

It must be frustrating to date a person with an Inflation Fetish. You're never going to be able to give him what he really wants. You can make him his favorite meal, call just to say I love you, leave romantic notes beneath his pillow in the morning, send naked jpegs to his private email account during the day, but it won't matter. You'll never be able to make your breasts expand to the size of medicine balls. You'll never find a way to fill yourself so full of helium that you float off into the atmosphere. And you'll never find a piece of magic gum that causes your internal organs to produce so much blueberry juice that your skin turns indigo and you blow up into a giant spherical piece of human fruit. Just not gonna happen. A large piece of your partner's sex life will forever exist solely in his mind.

Inflation Fetishists enjoy watching or reading about or hearing about or fantasizing about people expanding in impossible, physics-defying ways. Sometimes it's just body parts—usually breasts and butts, but in the world of fantasy anything is possible—and very often it's full-body expansion. The agent of change is rarely blood and tissue. (This isn't the same thing as wanting a person to get gi-freaking-gantically fat.) These fantasies have a more magical quality.

Inflation fetishists dream of witnessing a person—usually a woman—expand to ridiculous proportions, filled up with air or helium or cranberry cocktail. More often than not, the process of expansion is more exciting than the end result. They fantasize about seeing a woman's chest hiss and groan as it fills with air. Maybe in their little make-believe scenario, they're they ones subjecting the poor human blow-up toy to the experience, through a pump or magic spell or fizzy tablet. The moment of the *pop*—seeing the girl explode into a thousand cartoony balloon-like shreds—is often the orgasmic moment.

Of course, there's also the flip side: people who get off on imagining themselves blowing up. They enjoy the pretend feeling of transformation from something normal into something extraordinary. Obviously, they can't actually experience this. But they can try. Some go so far as to squeeze into special latex suits attached to air pumps and walk around their houses looking like those promotional air dolls that get stuck outside used car dealerships.

You'll never find a way
to fill yourself so full of
helium that you float off
into the atmosphere.

PSYCHOLOGICAL ORIGINS

This fetish is very similar to both the Schediaphilia (page 120) and Balloon Fetish (page 86). On one hand, it is a primarily fantasy-based, somewhat-cartoonish fetish that sometimes involves a pretty goofy-looking suit that you probably wouldn't want your friends to find hanging in your closet. And on the other hand, it involves the allure of inflatables, their sounds and smells and ability to pop. As with both, its roots are in the childhood innocence of imagination.

Some go so far as to squeeze into special latex suits attached to air pumps.

CONSIDERATIONS

Do not actually attempt to blow up a person using an electric air pump. It just . . . isn't a good idea.

Of Note . . .

The Inflation Fetish actually has nothing to do with comparing the values of two sets of goods at two separate points in time and then computing the value increase irrespective of any quality increase. Sorry. That's more of an econometric fetish; maybe you should go look for a financial mathematics dating site or something.

MACROPHILIA

The desire for a big, big, big love.

USEFUL ACCOUTREMENTS

- beautiful woman
- mad scientist
- atomic Expando Beam

THE FANTASY

You crane your neck upwards and nod. Yes, you say, you're familiar with Diane Arbus's work. God, is she going to keep on talking forever? You'd think with all the oxygen it must take to fill her lungs, she'd at least stop to take a breath. But no. Now she's on to Alexey Brodovitch and the Russian aesthetic. Who'd have guessed that such a big woman could be so full of small opinions? If you slipped away, would she even notice? Can she even see you way down here?

It wouldn't be so bad if she'd at least had the good taste to be honest on her profile. On her Nerve page, she'd stated that she was over 200 feet tall. Sure, she's over 200 feet. Like, 300 feet over. Certainly, there are men out there who are interested in a 500-foot woman. You're just not one of them. 250 feet, you can handle, but this is a bit much. Now you're gonna have to feign interest for a few hours and then make some lame excuse about why you're not in the mood to get pummeled tonight. Why don't giantesses just tell the truth on their profiles? This isn't good for anyone concerned.

Not like that incredible date you had with that curvy little 175-foot gal. Those giant toes she let you rub up and down on, grrrr. Now *she* was a minx . . .

WHAT IS IT?

You're probably not going to wake up tomorrow morning to find a 300-foot supermodel in a makeshift football-field tarp bikini stomping through your city, tearing apart buildings with her finely manicured hands and smashing buses beneath her hugely dainty feet. Not to say it's completely out of the realm of possibility. But the odds are against it. So, if you're into Macrophilia, you're most likely going to have to find other ways of satisfying your particular fantasy.

You can do what most Macrophiles do, which is surf the Internet for Macrophile porn featuring models (female and male) Photoshopped into cityscapes or beside mountains. Because the source material is often taken from the *Sports Illustrated Swimsuit Issue* or *Playgirl*, the giantesses and giants of these photo-manipulations usually seem less interested in destroying civilization than in lounging around and posing for normal-sized people's enjoyment. However, because a large part of the Macrophile's fantasy is to be squashed or devoured by an extremely plus-sized person, you will also be able to find a number of images showing puny men being lowered, grape-style, into a beautiful woman's tremendous mouth (Vorarephilia, page 196) or being rubbed into nothingness between her fingers.

If that doesn't do it for you, another option is to find an actual real-life giantess or giant and somehow convince him or her to squash you. Unfortunately, the tallest living man, Xi Shun of China, is only 7'9", and the tallest living woman, Sandy Allen of Indiana, a mere 7'7". That's probably not gonna cut it for a hardcore Macrophile.

PSYCHOLOGICAL ORIGINS

The desire to be destroyed at the hands (or feet, or teeth) of a gigantic person is, rather obviously, a submissive one. The bearer of the fantasy is most likely wrestling with feelings of inadequacy. Or, because he or she feels inadequate, can only imagine sexuality when it is from a power being wielded against him or her (almost always a him).

In some instances, a Macrophile may fantasize about being the giant. In such a case, the fantasy is almost certainly that of gaining power. Again, probably because of a perceived lack of genuine power in real life.

CONSIDERATIONS

Should the day ever come that your hometown is attacked by a towering Playboy model, just let that Macrophile buddy of yours go and get yourself to safety. 'Cause, man, he's already gone.

> ## *Of Note . . .*
>
> Macrophilia has a cousin in Microphilia, in which a person fantasizes about being shrunk down to a tiny size and then squashed, eaten, or otherwise abused by a regular-sized person. The physics are slightly different, but the result is pretty much the same.

SCHEDIAPHILIA
(ALSO TOONOPHILIA, YIFF)

The insatiable lust for pencil and ink.

USEFUL ACCOUTREMENTS

○ paper
○ pencil

○ ink
○ hand lotion

THE FANTASY

You're barely through the door before she's bounding across the room into your arms, leaving nothing but a fox-girl-shaped puff of smoke lingering above her reading chair. The discarded book hovers in space for a brief moment, and by the time it hits the floor, she's pawing her way up and down your body, licking you with passionate enthusiasm. "Baby," you say, "let me at least get inside."

"I can't help it," she says, batting her three-inch-long lashes over her saucer-sized eyes. "I missed you." She smiles, showing a mouth full of sharp teeth. She is beautiful—pointed ears, delicately long snout, and the finest, softest golden fur you've ever seen grace a woman's face.

But suddenly her expression changes, eyes narrowing, ears raised toward the ceiling. "What's this?" she asks, grabbing at the collar of your shirt. Oh no! How could you have been so stupid? "Is this . . . ? Is this . . . ? Is this hygroscopic slime?!" Her eyes dart out into angry daggers, nearly stabbing into your cheek, and you can see the beginning wisps of steam trickling out from her ears. Why? Why did you put all of this at risk for one afternoon's dalliance with a tawdry slug girl?

WHAT IS IT?

As you probably already know, cartoon characters are vastly superior to real people in practically every way. They can fall off of a cliff without dying. Withstand an explosion and remain in one piece. Take an anvil right to the head with only the slightest of brain trauma. Some of them can fly. Others can disappear in a puff of smoke. And, anatomically, they are in no way hampered by the annoyance of gravity. Hourglass-shaped women walk confidently on microscopic feet. Breasts bulge out a yard or two before their chests. And you could wrap a wristwatch around their waists. Twice. As for the men, they've been known to sport phalluses so large they could warp time and space. Are they in any way inferior to real people? Well, besides the fact that they're not real? Actually, that could be considered a plus as well.

Hence, it should come as no surprise that something like Schediaphilia—the sexual attraction to cartoon characters—has emerged. There's just so darn much to find attractive.

In the world of Furry Fandom, some people have chosen to make the make-believe world of cartoons their primary existence. They create anthropomorphic "fursona" characters for themselves, usually modeled after some sort of animal. In some instances, these characters become as important as their real lives. Wanna be a half-man/half-wolf who flies around in a spaceship shaped like a toaster oven making conjugal visits across the universe? Why not? If it can be imagined, it can be drawn.

You can meet other people who are into this online, in fursona, chat about stuff and, on occasion, get yiffy. "Yiff" is a term for role-playing sex between two anthropomorphic fursonas. (Take a minute, breathe, continue reading when your head stops spinning.) Like the word "smurf" to the Smurfs, it's kind of an all-purpose word, meaning just about anything sexual. Yiff, because it occurs mostly through texting and imagination, can get pretty seriously hardcore. Sometimes, it extends to Vorarephilia (page 196).

PSYCHOLOGICAL ORIGINS

You know, there hasn't been a whole lot of research into this phenomenon. But you can probably figure it has something to do with childhood memories and lack of self-esteem. Many furry fans have mentioned Bugs Bunny's cross-dressing episodes as an influence.

CONSIDERATIONS

Schediaphilia is about as safe as fetishes come, physically speaking. Psychologically, however, idealizing imaginatively drawn cartoon characters may promote some body image issues.

Of Note . . .

Yiffers, like other members of Furry Fandom, meet often at conventions and bring their fantasy lives into reality with the aid of specially made fursona costumes. No, really. (See Fursuit Fetish, page 168.)

SPECTROPHILIA

The feeling that you need spectral healing.

USEFUL ACCOUTREMENTS

- O   mirror
- O   Ouija board
- O   condom with ectoplasmicide

THE FANTASY

You cannot see him, you cannot hear him, but you can feel his presence. He's in the room with you. A shiver runs down your spine as the delicate static charge of his fingers traces its way from the hollow of your neck to the curve of your breast. You sense weightless fingers pull away the straps of your nightgown until they're sliding down your forearms and past your fingertips. The silk garment falls to a bundle at your feet, and you think that you may swoon before you're lifted gently from the ground and held aloft by invisibly powerful arms. You throw your head back in abandon. In anticipation. And then, the bedroom doorknob turns, the door creaks open . . .

"Oh, jeez!" an unseen voice mutters quickly. You fall to the floor, landing hard on your tailbone.

"Why are you naked?" your husband asks.

"Um. I was doing yoga," you say.

"Oh," he says and scratches his stomach. "Do we have any more mustard?"

WHAT IS IT?

Spectrophilia, or sex with otherworldly beings, is currently the most popular form of sex in the world. It's just that most people don't realize it's happening. See, while you're asleep, an incubus (male demon spirit) or a succubus (female demon spirit) floats through your wall—because they don't have to use doors—climbs on top of you, and pleasures his or herself. This is what causes nightmares. Next time you wake up suddenly, dripping sweat, your heart racing, you can say to yourself, "I just got raped by a ghost!" (Note: The reference for this is approximately 500 years old, so you may want to double-check that explanation.)

That's all well and good for those put off by the idea of incorporeal coitus. But what about the people who *want* to feel the cold hand of death groping them beneath the sheets, whose fantasies are haunted by ethereal phalluses or phantasmal breasts? What about all those diehard Spectrophiliacs out there? Where will they find satisfaction?

They have their work cut out for them, to be sure. Ghosts, demons, angels, and demigods are notorious for playing hard to get. They pop up when they want to pop up, and then disappear without even leaving a note. They don't return your phone calls. You can try hanging out in cemeteries and haunted houses, but usually you just end up feeling cheapened. Sister, give it up and move on with your life. You don't need no ghost to feel complete.

One thing that unsatisfied Spectrophiliacs can do is engage in mirror play with a non-ghost partner. Viewing an erotic image via reflection can simulate the experience of interacting with an apparitional being. Many ghost lovers swear by it.

PSYCHOLOGICAL ORIGINS

The body's reactions to fear and sexual excitement are very similar to one another. Both include increased blood pressure, shortness of breath, and hypersensitivity. This is one of the reasons why it's often the thing that most frightens you that you tend to fetishize. Ghosts are the unknown. The unknown is scary. Scary is sexy. Ergo, ghosts are sexy.

CONSIDERATIONS

Ghosts are not known to carry venereal diseases, nor can they get you pregnant, so it's really the safest sex you can have. However, if you're caught having sex with a ghost, you're likely to be burned at the stake.

Of Note . . .

According to the *Malleus Maleficarum*, essentially a witch hunter's bible published way back in the super-enlightened 15th century, ghosts "seem chiefly to molest women and girls with beautiful hair; either . . . because they are boastfully vain about it, or because God in His goodness permits this so that women may be afraid to entice men by the very means by which the devils wish them to entice men."

Of course, there may be some ghosts who dig ugly hair and just don't want to admit it. So it's hard to say.

FLORA & FAUNA

CRUSH FETISH

The fantasy of being squashed like the disgusting little bug you know you are.

USEFUL ACCOUTREMENTS

○ bugs
○ shoes
○ feet

THE FANTASY

You're a worm. Just a dirty little worm, disgusting and repulsive. What self-respecting woman would want to soil the soles of her designer wedges to put you out of your grotesque misery? What elegant female creature would even consider your existence long enough to step down upon your squirming Lumbrical body, pushing harder and harder until you can feel the pressure of your internal organs rising up into your head and erupting onto the warm cement of the sidewalk?

Oh, but if you ever do meet her, you'll marry that woman for certain.

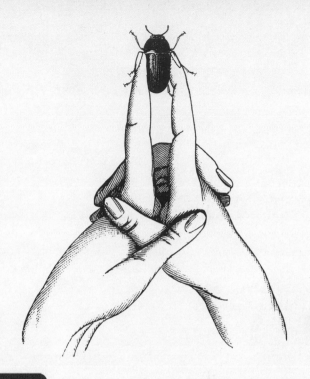

WHAT IS IT?

The Crush Fetish is the sexual gratification of watching a woman stepping on small creatures—whether in bare feet, high heels, Nikes, combat boots, ballet shoes, or fuzzy slippers. Typically, the small creatures are bugs, worms, roaches, spiders, and so forth. But small mammals, such as mice, rats, and rabbits, will also satisfy. The scenario can be achieved by coercing a woman to do it for you, by purchasing or downloading the (in)appropriate videos, or simply through fantasy.

In most cases, the Crush Fetishist—or Crush Freak, as they're often called—will imagine himself (and they're nearly always men, because men are just incredibly level-headed when it comes to sex) as the crushed animal. Often, they'll enjoy the fantasy of being helpless and worthless. They enjoy dirty talk along the lines of, "I am totally going to squoosh you with my big foot," and "I am totally going to use my big foot to squoosh you."

PSYCHOLOGICAL ORIGINS

The Crush Fetish is actually a cocktail of several other fetishes. Take equal parts Podophilia (page 68), Macrophilia (page 116), and Entomophilia (page 142), and maybe a splash of Retifism (page 98). Shake well and smash underneath the heel of a woman's foot.

Why would people actually enjoy watching defenseless animals being tortured and killed? It might be that this is a way for people to deal with feelings of inadequacy or weakness, either by watching how something less powerful than them is treated, or by actually identifying with the powerless thing and vicariously experiencing the violent spectacle. Or it might just be that people are weirdoes.

They enjoy dirty talk along the lines of, "I am totally going to use my big foot to squoosh you."

The actual practice of crushing vertebrate animals for sexual gratification is illegal. Unless the vertebrate animal is killed so as to be made into a coat, a shoe, or an expensive dinner that will be used or bartered with the intent of eventually leading to sexual gratification indirectly. That middle part makes all the difference.

Of Note . . .

A Chinese woman, dubbed the kitten killer of Hangzhou, caused a great deal of controversy after she was videotaped wearing elegant evening attire and killing a kitten with the heel of a stiletto shoe. Once the videotape was released to the Internet, people fell all over themselves watching it again and again in disgust to show how much they hated watching it.

FLORA & FAUNA

DENDROPHILIA
(ALSO ARBORPHILIA, PHYTOPHILIA)

The overwhelming urge to get some wood.

USEFUL ACCOUTREMENTS

- O trees
- O ferns
- O bushes
- O shrubs

THE FANTASY

She was an elegant little conifer. A juniper, most likely. You'd had too much whiskey; you didn't know what you were thinking. From your campsite, you heard her calling: "Come to me. Nobody has to know. It'll be our little secret." So you crawled from your sleeping bag and followed the path back to where you'd first locked eyes on the gentle curves of her thin trunk. Dropping your clothes in a pile at her feet, you climbed into her enveloping limbs, her echinulate leaves digging into your naked flesh.

As beautiful as it was, you're sorry for having done it. Because now your sweet, loving oak, the one with which you've made your home, sits alone, bowed in the backyard. You can't bring yourself to face her. Will she be able to smell the sap?

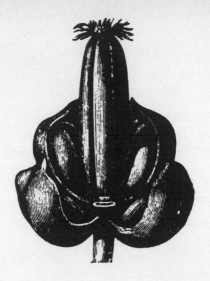

WHAT IS IT?

Sex and vegetation got themselves all mixed up together in people's minds millennia ago, and now it seems practically impossible to disentangle them completely. However, while most people draw the line at courting their lovers with flowers, and perhaps engaging in the occasional stimulating aloe rubdown, some take it a bit further. Quite a bit further. Like, all the way to fourth base.

To a Dendrophiliac, trees are sexual objects. Their leaves are soft and enveloping; their branches, long and hard. Peel away the bark of an adolescent tree and you'll find a smooth, moist, almost flesh-like texture that welcomes the touch but does not give too easily. And if you're lucky enough to come across a trunk with a conveniently placed hole, well, come on; that tree is asking for it.

Dendrophiliacs have been known to become quite attached to their tree-loves, fashioning artificial vaginas from their leaves, and speaking tenderly and romantically to them while stroking their bark. Should you find yourself sufficiently captivated by just such a tall, strong partner, you might even be moved to adopt a seedling as your own child.

PSYCHOLOGICAL ORIGINS

Not to go out on a limb (apologies), but true Dendrophilia, beyond simply looking for new textures with which to experiment, may be the result of a deep-seeded (more apologies) emotional love for nature that blossoms (even more apologies) into something much greater.

> The coarse caress of your lover's bark may feel stimulating in the heat of the moment.

First off, you should note that tree sap is a real bitch to get out of your hair, so proceed with caution. Chafing is also a concern. While the coarse caress of your lover's bark may feel stimulating in the heat of the moment, if you're not careful you could walk away with some nasty burns. And while sexually transmitted diseases are not an issue per se, you should protect yourself against splinters, insects, squirrels, and other inhabitants, and potential irritants like poison oak.

Also, this should be obvious, but it's worth noting: discretion is key. Your feelings toward a tree may seem pure and true to you, but the unenlightened may think otherwise.

Of Note . . .

The film *The Evil Dead*, by Sam Raimi, contains probably the most overt depiction of Dendrophilia. In it, a female character played by Ellen Sandweiss becomes an unwilling participant in Dendrophilia with some bewitched foliage, which wraps her, bondage-style, in its vines and then does unprintable things with its branches.

DORAPHILIA

The attraction to skin or fur not of your sexual partner.

USEFUL ACCOUTREMENTS

- ○ mink coat
- ○ fox stole
- ○ leather vest
- ○ suede shoes

THE FANTASY

Wow! Could you believe the look on her face when she opened the gift box? Fur coats may be a bit outmoded these days, but there's a classic elegance to them that will never truly be lost. She's positively glowing! She's thrilled! Oh, man, you are in!

Just think, if she's this happy for a coat, imagine her reaction when you bring her back to your bedroom. She will absolutely flip when she sees the fur-lined sheets. And the fur-lined pillows. And the fur-lined headboard. The fur-lined dresser, the fur-lined wardrobe, the fur-lined full-length mirror, the fur-lined door, the fur-lined floor, the fur-lined radiator.

Oh, man, this is it. You're finally gonna get to use the fur-lined condoms!

WHAT IS IT?

You know that mink coat you keep in the closet? The one you pull out just for those special nights when you want to feel extra sexy? Or that leather collar you keep tucked in your bag? You know, the one that you discreetly fasten around your neck before climbing into bed with somebody because you like the way it rubs against your skin when you sweat? Or that antelope pelt you keep stuffed down your pants? Those are all aspects of your Doraphilia!

DORAPHILIA

Doraphilia is not simply the enjoyment of wearing furs or leather or other animal skins. If that were the case, more than half of the people in world would be Doraphiliacs. Which would mean you were weird if you *weren't* a Doraphiliac. Rather, Doraphilia is a fetish for the hide or coat of an animal. For the true Doraphilac, leather or fur or what-have-you is an absolutely necessary part of the sexual act. Whether it's stroked or rubbed against beforehand for stimulation, worn upon the body during, or made the object of sexual attention itself, you gotta have the skin.

PSYCHOLOGICAL ORIGINS

What's behind this fascination for wearing dead animals? The answer is uncertain and complex. It could be that the texture or smell of a hide makes you feel imbued with the energy of the animal it came from, which can be either invigorating or calming. Humans have been wrapping themselves in other animals for thousands of years. You can imagine how it must have affected your ancestors. On one hand, it made them feel safe; fur kept them warm and protected from the elements. On the other hand, it was a patent trophy of dominance over another living creature. We all know humans love that shit.

The only things, as a Doraphiliac, that you really need to watch out for are those annoying animal rights protestors. Blah blah blah, an animal died so that you can have a weird fetish orgasm, boo hoo hoo. If you actually care about all that nonsense, you can try to make the switch to faux-fur or faux-leather accoutrements, which are typically made out of tofu and do not provide nearly the same gratifying sense of dominance over nature (though tofu can be surprisingly aggressive in the wild).

Of Note . . .

Leopold von Sacher-Masoch, the Austrian author of *Venus in Furs*, was not only a Doraphiliac (he supposedly stroked a fur at his writing desk)—he was also the masochist for whom masochism is named. Interestingly, the Doraphilic interest in leather went on to become one of the most prominent aspects of BDSM, in which it's been used for chaps, vests, hats, boots, whips, bindings, blindfolds, leashes, and just about anything else people can think of to make out of it.

FLORA & FAUNA

ENTOMOPHILIA
(ALSO FORMICOPHILIA)

The joy of insects.

USEFUL ACCOUTREMENTS

- ○ anthill
- ○ wasp's nest
- ○ beehive
- ○ roach motel

THE FANTASY

It's an odd sensation, pulling home into the driveway while it's still daylight. You turn off the engine and step out of the car with a rumbling dread in your stomach. You couldn't bring yourself to call your wife from the office; the word "downsized" seems so much more shameful through the tinny whine of a telephone receiver. You enter the house and head for the bedroom. A short reprieve from the inevitable? Maybe. Maybe a quick romp will clear your mind, help you think of a way to break the news more happily. Maybe some small sliver of light will make itself visible.

As you reach the bedroom, you notice a sound coming from under the door. It almost sounds like—well, like singing. Yes, there it is, it's definitely a song, and it's definitely your wife's voice. As you pause, curious, the song grows louder, and louder, until you can distinctly make out the childhood tune:

The ants go marching one by one, hurrah, hurrah.

The ants go marching one by one, hur—ahh. Ooh. Yeah. Hur-ahhhhhh . . .

Throwing open the door to reveal your wife naked in bed, clutching your upturned ant farm with a grin of pure rapture, your workday troubles are immediately replaced by a warm sensation below the belt.

"Hi hon. Is there room in bed for one more?" you ask. "Hurrah, indeed!"

WHAT IS IT?

Cockroaches. Water bugs. Spiders. Scorpions. Flies. Mosquitoes. Bees. Wasps. Hornets. Ants. Crickets. Earthworms. Caterpillars. Silverfish. Centipedes. Millipedes. Yeah, millipedes . . . All those legs. All those tiny insectoid feet. Can't you just imagine the sensation of them scuttling across your soft flesh? Can you think of anything sexier than looking down at your naked body and seeing a swarm of insects crawling this way and that way and down this slope and up this precipice? Not if you're an Entomophiliac, you can't.

Entomophilia is the use of bugs for sexual pleasure. It's related, somewhat, to Zoophilia (page 146), except that in this case, you can't really argue that you're having sex with the non-human life form in question. There's no question of the insects being consenting partners; they're blatantly being objectified. Plus, it's pretty difficult to enter into genuine coitus with a fruit fly.

Some Entomophiliacs simply enjoy the stimulation derived from an ant's random wandering about the skin, or from watching it wander about their partner's. Others enjoy the charge of pain from a spider's bite. Some even purposefully induce a bee's sting on the penis, as it causes swelling and is said to increase sexual pleasure and endurance.

PSYCHOLOGICAL ORIGINS

Entomophilia may stem from one of two causes. On one hand, there's the whole dominance-over-helpless-living-creatures thing. Insects are tiny and crushable and when you invite them into bed, all they can really do is run around tickling you, and if that feels good, well, consider them your sexual slaves. On the other hand, insects are totally creepy and gross, and if a traumatic experience in childhood instilled in you a healthy fear of bugs, that fear can sometimes blur into excitement and arousal.

Insects carry a multitude of diseases; from malaria to Lyme Disease to the Black Plague, an insect can give it to you. No, not every fly or mosquito that lands on you is going to make you sick, so you can take your chances if so inclined. However, this book is officially anti-advising the use of bugs for sex, mostly for hygienic reasons, but also because bugs have it bad enough without your shameless advances.

Of Note . . .

A man walks into a doctor's office and says, "Doc, I'm having trouble urinating." The doctor examines him and discovers a blockage in his urethra. "We're going to have to operate," the doctor says. So, he operates and pulls from the man's urinary tract a clump of calcified beetles. He says to the man, "Do you know how these beetles got in your urinary tract?" The man thinks for a moment and says, "Maybe it's from all those times I hung out at the local golf course with the express purpose of finding beetles to stick in there so that I could get off." (Not a great punch line, but a true story.)

FLORA & FAUNA

ZOOPHILIA
(ALSO ZOOSEXUALITY, BESTIALITY)

The desire to have sexual relations with dogs, sheep, sheepdogs, and . . . pretty much any animal.

USEFUL ACCOUTREMENTS

- horse
- cow
- dolphin
- sheep
- goldfish

THE FANTASY

Your car has broken down on a desolate country road in the dead of night, so you make your way on foot to the only light for miles—a humble, teetering farmhouse you passed before sundown. Cautiously, you knock on the front door and a grizzled old man answers. Hat in hand, you ask for a place to sleep. The old man informs you that there's not an inch of space in the house, but you're welcome to bed down in the barn.

The barn! Could it be? Your heart races, but you do your best to remain calm as the old man leads you out back to a musty hay-strewn lean-to filled with the sweet smell of its inhabitants. After he has left you alone, you drop your bag and race around, searching for the one you'd seen. There she is! Standing coolly in the corner, chewing her cud, just as beautiful as she was when you'd seen her in the field.

You were too nervous, too shy, to stop the car and approach her the first time. But now, fate has brought you together, and you won't make the same mistake twice. You take a deep breath and step forward. Toward her, and toward the single most spectacular night of your life . . .

WHAT IS IT?

Zoophilia is the love—both romantic and sexual—of non-human animals. In most human cultures, it's frowned upon. However, in non-human cultures, it's hardly even discussed. Though possibly because most animals lack the capacity of speech, it may owe to the fact that to those not hampered by human prudishness, it's simply not a big deal.

A good rule of thumb for considering whether to engage in sexual relations of all types and formations is, so long as it occurs between two consenting adults, all's fair. This rule becomes slightly more complicated when one of the adults is an animal. Can an animal technically give consent? Some say yes; most say no. Then again, most people don't want to have sex with animals, so they're probably not giving the matter a ton of consideration. Many Zoophiliacs do want to. If you find yourself troubled by the whole consent issue, just think of it this way: Remember the last time you visited your friend's house and his Dalmatian climbed up behind you on the couch and started getting intimate with the small of your back? Does that sound like a prude unwilling to grant you the green light?

The practice of human-on-animal (or animal-on-human) copulation is likely as old as the human race itself. In fact, it's believed by some anthropologists that 6.3 million years ago, when humans and apes became evolutionarily separate species, they just couldn't let go of the sweet love they knew in those halcyon days when they shared a common genetic makeup. You know—old habits die hard. And, as human civilization grew more sophisticated, the practice continued. In some herding communities, it was even considered "just one of those things" that a reckless and romantic adolescent goes through before settling down with a boring human partner.

In our modern Western culture, though, Zoophilia has generally been considered sinful and grotesque. It wasn't until the 1960s that psychological professionals began to consider—and ultimately conclude—that there maybe isn't anything technically "wrong" with engaging in sexual activity with another species. They even went so far as to posit that it might be a legitimate human sexual orientation, which can be measured along a scale similar to Kinsey's heterosexual-homosexual scale. A number of self-professed (though anonymous) Zoophiles have made their best effort to forward this viewpoint, going so far as to present their own human-animal experiences as loving, mutually-consenting relationships. Zoophilia was, in fact, removed from the newest edition of the *Diagnostic and Statistical Manual of Mental Disorders*, along with homosexuality.

> The practice of human-on-animal (or animal-on-human) copulation is likely as old as the human race itself.

CONSIDERATIONS

If you are going to have sex with an animal, you should educate yourself on what you have in store. For example, the head of a male dog's penis will swell to several times its size during orgasm. Worth noting, too, is that a dolphin's ejaculate comes out quite forcefully, and can travel up to fourteen yards if unobstructed.

And if you're planning to have sex with a lion, for God's sake, let him or her lead.

Of Note . . .

While there are no accurate statistics for Zoophilia due to its illegality and stigma, you can rest assured it's far more common in modern society than you probably think. In the summer of 2005, to cite just one instance, a Seattle man died while engaged in physical relations with a horse. And a quick search for "Zoophilia" on Google produces hundreds of thousands of hits, yielding an untold number of stories of man-and-beast unions.

COSTUMES & PLAY

AGALMATOPHILIA
(ALSO STATUEPHILIA, PYGMALIONISM)

The "appreciation" of Classical sculpture.

USEFUL ACCOUTREMENTS

- head of a Gorgon sister
- King Midas's touch
- body paint
- Photoshop

THE FANTASY

She beautiful. She's perfect. Why, she's the most amazing being you've ever seen! It's inconceivable, really, that she was born of a chunk of lifeless marble. Could a mere man have chiseled such exquisite limbs? Such fragile little fingers and supple toes? And that face, so regal, so wise . . . No artist born was ever so talented. Would it not be easier to believe that an ancient princess happened unawares into the path of some horrid beast, under whose gaze she found herself turned to stone before even the fear could set in?

And if it were so, would it in fact be a pity to have such a woman frozen for all eternity? Nay, it was fate! For how could the gods allow an object of such magnificence to deteriorate and waste away into the earth? Is it not most fitting that she should inspire men for all the ages? Is it not a pure and joyous thing that she should stand before you now? Is it not awesome to rub your pecker up against her thigh? Oh, that's it . . . That's the spot.

WHAT IS IT?

Some people might complain that their partner is cold, hard, and unfeeling in bed, or that they just lay there, unmoving, during sex. But maybe, just maybe, what those people need is an introduction to the joys of Agalmatophilia. You have not experienced the full grandeur of erotic love until you've fondled a pair of smooth, unyielding alabaster breasts. Or kissed a pert, shimmering bronze mouth and pulled away with a mineral taste still lingering on your tongue. Or run your finger down the length of a cool marble ass crack. Statue sex is not to be compared!

To be fair, most Agalmatophiles don't spend their nights molesting statuary. That's merely the fantasy. Instead, they may simply rely on a whole lot of body paint and hours of standing very, very still.

COSTUMES & PLAY

In some cases, one partner will climb into a body-fitting statue cast (see Mummification Fetish, page 172) to enhance the sensation. Usually, though, an Agalmatophile will simply pleasure himself to pictures of naked women Photoshopped to look like statues or mannequins.

The fetish is called Pygmalionism by some because of its relation to the classic Greek myth of Pygmalion, who sculpted his perfect woman from pure white ivory, only to see her turned into living flesh by Aphrodite, the goddess of love. Whatever name it goes by, role-playing tends to be a big part of Agalmatophilia. Let's say you've procured the head of the slain Gorgon sister, which you wield before your love to freeze her in place. Now this person is stuck, petrified into some unlikely suggestive position, yours to do whatever you wish until a magical antidote is administered. Think of the possibilities!

PSYCHOLOGICAL ORIGINS

Agalmatophilia came into its current popularity along with the Robofetish (page 188) and a mind control fetish on the *alt.sex.fetish.robots* Internet newsgroup, and all three have a lot in common. Most notably, at their heart, all three are very light forms of BDSM, satisfying followers' needs for submission or dominance during sex. Agalmatophilia is bondage without binding. And what it lacks in make-believe violence, it makes up for in real-life geekiness.

CONSIDERATIONS

If you do decide to go all out and make sweet, hard love to a real statue, you'd be wise to find a less public place than the average museum, city park, or national monument. In his book *Psychopathia Sexualis*, Richard von Krafft-Ebing recounts the incident of a gardener who fell in love with an outdoor statue of Venus de Milo and was caught in the act of gardener-statuary bliss. Which is not only bad for business but also just trashy; he could have at least sprung for a hotel room.

Of Note . . .

In a certain sense, Agalmatophilia can also be thought of as related to both Necrophilia (page 64) and the phenomenon of reality television, as all three concern an attraction to objects that resemble people but are, in fact, lifeless ciphers.

COULROPHILIA
(ALSO CLOWN FETISH)

The desire to fit as many sex partners as possible into a tiny car.

USEFUL ACCOUTREMENTS

- red nose
- grease paint
- big floppy shoes
- novelty handcuffs

THE FANTASY

It's almost closing time and the crowd is thinning out. Two by two, the patrons are shimmying into thick wool coats and leaving small piles of cash beneath empty bottles of beer. The bartender nods as they walk toward the door and out into a cold rain that falls like lost dreams. And thus, the bar is two souls lonelier.

You glance sideways to see if the middle-aged man with arms lined in ink and hair slicked with grease has gotten any more attractive with your last bourbon. He hasn't, and you steel yourself for another night of watching headlights slip across the walls of your sagging apartment.

The front door clatters open. A man walks in and pulls off a sopping wet straw hat. Bright rainbow curls pour down about his cheeks. His pale round face seems forlorn as his eyes dart quickly about the room and finally settle on the barkeep. "The usual, Bubbles?" One beep of the nose for yes, and he opens up his down-turned smile of a mouth to toss back a shot of liquor. He's a sad clown. Exactly your type. Suddenly, your evening just got a lot more jolly.

WHAT IS IT?

Coulrophilia is a sexual attraction to clowns. You know, those incredibly sexy people with the huge bulging feet and the luscious ruby red noses. Can't you just feel your blood pressure rising at the thought of staring deep into a perpetually smiling face as the naughty harlequin rubs his joy buzzers all over your naked flesh? You've been a bad, bad circusgoer. You deserve a pie right in the face. But you'd probably like that, wouldn't you?

COSTUMES & PLAY

COULROPHILIA

If you want in on this hot clown action, the first order of business is to dress the part. You and your partner should track down colorful wigs, face paint, novelty shoes, bright suspenders, and red noses, put all of it on, and then go at it. Some Coulrophiliacs like to slap each other with cream pies, squirt seltzer into each other's faces, or hit each other with squeaky hammers. Some clown fetishists kick it up a notch, incorporating S&M (see Sadomasochism, page 10) into the play. Imagine being tied to a bondage rack and slapped repeatedly . . . with a rubber chicken.

PSYCHOLOGICAL ORIGINS

Why would anybody do this? Because it's fun! Coulrophilia adds a level of silliness to sex. Who doesn't love a clown? Well, besides the millions of people who are completely horrified by them. You know, the people with Coulro*phobia*. Because the human sex drive is what it is, however, many of the same people who are deathly afraid of clowns are the ones who want to have sex with them. As in many other fetishes, confronting one's fears can be arousing. People are funny. Clowns are (sorta) funny. It works out.

Why would anybody do this? Because it's fun! Coulrophilia adds a level of silliness to sex.

CONSIDERATIONS

If you're going to get into Coulrophilia, you might want to learn the proper way to pratfall. (It's all fun and games until somebody breaks a bone.) Also, this cannot be stressed enough: Never hit your lover with a pie fresh out of the oven. Let it cool first. He or she will thank you.

Of Note . . .

Ouchy the Clown, a professional S&M clown dominant, is known Internet-wide for his friendly-but-firm approach and wide array of services, including conflict resolution, professional DJ-ing, and pubic hair grooming. Look him up!

COSTUMES & PLAY

FORNIPHILIA
(ALSO HUMAN FURNITURE)

The desire to live the life of a curio cabinet.

USEFUL ACCOUTREMENTS

- cushions
- throw pillows
- slip cover

THE FANTASY

Isn't this just the sexiest knick-knack display case you've ever laid eyes on? Couldn't you just place baubles and gimcracks upon its finely shaped shelves all night long? The porcelain coy fairy would look so lovely right . . . here. Oh yeah, that's the spot. Mmmmmm . . .

This bride and groom salt and pepper set will go right . . . here and . . . here. And what about this Wilmington, Delaware snow globe, where should that go? Find a good spot. Find the *perfect* spot. How about . . . right . . . *heeeeerrrre*. Oh, that's it! The knick-knack display case likes that, doesn't it?

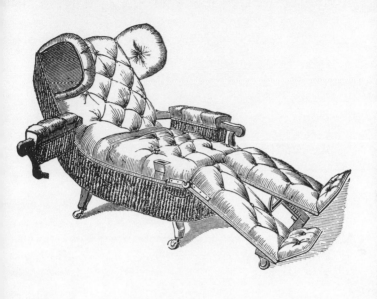

WHAT IS IT?

When was the last time you came home from work and asked the coffee table how its day was and then took it to the Olive Garden for a much deserved shrimp and asparagus risotto? Probably not in a long time. But what if your coffee table was your wife? Or your wife was your coffee table?

Pro-feminist social activists have spent tireless decades trying to push back the flood of the objectification of women—and, in some cases, men—that seems to be a byproduct of modern life, reasoning that to objectify a model or actor is to strip that person of her or his humanity. However, it appears that that's exactly what some people want: to be objectified. To be an object. And you can't get much more object-y than a piece of furniture—a table, a chair, a lamp, a hat rack, an entertainment center . . . This is the crux of Forniphilia.

Practicing it can be as simple as lying on the floor like a rug or kneeling on all fours with a glass top resting on your shoulder blades and butt, or it can get quite a bit more sophisticated. Some Forniphiliacs have managed to make their partners into chandeliers, easy chairs, and other complex forms. In these cases, there's a lot of bondage involved, and if you decide to embark upon the life of human furniture you may find yourself tied up in all sorts of awkward positions. Legs spread wide with light bulbs dangling from your ankles. Feet suspended above your head and backs of your thighs laid flat as the seat of a chair. And then what? And then, nothing. You sit there being a chair. Chairs don't move. They don't talk. And they certainly don't get tired and have to use the bathroom.

Forniphilia is an extreme form of BDSM. For the furniture, it allows them to push submissiveness toward its outer limit. You're tied up. You're immobile. You're dehumanized. Some people find this to be the height of eroticism. And for the furniture user, it allows him or her to do just that: Use. Use another human being for something simple. Treat another human being as a thing.

Obviously, this is not for everyone, and to many it may seem repulsive. But the psychology behind treating a person as a futon is probably not as far from the way many people look at others in a dance club as one might like to admit. That girl you brought back to your hotel room during Spring Break in Cancun—how much of that was actually for her conversation?

> You're tied up. You're immobile. You're dehumanized. Some people find this to be the height of eroticism.

CONSIDERATIONS

One good thing about Forniphilia is that assembly does not require one of those little curvy wrench-things that hurt your fingers when you try to twist them. However, your Forniphiliac furniture really doesn't last very long. It can't. People, much like pressboard bookshelves, were not designed to be used as furniture for an extended period of time. If left in one position for too long—particularly the more awkward ones—blood circulation may be cut off. You should probably start with very short trials.

And never, ever, ever, ever leave a bound person alone, for any amount of time. Trust is absolutely essential in any extreme form of BDSM. The dominant partner should be on hand at all times to get the submissive out of his or her bindings the instant that discomfort—physical, psychological, or emotional—occurs.

And don't let the dog on the furniture! How many times do you have to be told? He leaves claw marks.

If you don't want to be a lamp,
you don't have to be a lamp. You
can be an end table.

Of Note . . .

In Susannah Breslin's short story "F is for Forniphilia," from her chapbook *You're a Bad Man,
Aren't You?*, a dutiful loving wife enacts the part
of a lamp for her husband's pleasure. "Her
husband was great. But he wanted his wife to
be different pieces of furniture, depending
on the day of the week. That was hard. For
her. It turned him on. She said out loud, 'I am
a lamp.' She didn't really want to be a lamp,
though. She wanted to be a human being. That
was the problem."

   The lesson you should pull from this story
is that if you don't want to be a lamp, you don't
have to be a lamp. You can be an end table. Or
a cabinet. Or a rug. Or even a person. It sounds
weird, but, hey, whatever turns you on.

FURSUIT FETISH

The desire to do it like a couple of cute and furry anthropomorphic animals.

USEFUL ACCOUTREMENTS

- an absolutely adorable full-size fuzzy animal costume
- condom

THE FANTASY

You see her from across the bar. Sipping a sea breeze from a straw through an SPH in her sexy feline head. You've always had a thing for cat girls. So poised. So aloof. So sexy. You turn sideways and peer straight ahead toward the mirror-lined wall. Oh, you look good. Damn good. You give yourself a quick reassuring *woof* and then turn back to the sexy cat. It's time to move in for the kill.

"Hey, kitty," you say, leaning on one paw against the bar counter. "They say cats and dogs are natural enemies. You wanna prove them wrong?"

"Um, I'm a dude," the sexy cat says.

"Whatever," you say. "Dogs aren't picky."

Listen, if you're into having sex with people while they're dressed up like big cuddly honey bears, it's nobody's business but your own. Or if your idea of a perfect evening is one spent riding atop a sexy bunny rabbit while staring lovingly into its vacuous plastic eyes, then good for you. And why should anyone care if you keep your own cute and fuzzy tiger costume, complete with monstrously large head and SPH (strategically placed hole), in your bedroom closet? You should relish your Fursuit Fetish and take pride in the fact that you've embraced what has to be one of the most interesting sexual proclivities ever dreamed up by humans.

And if you haven't gotten into the Fursuit scene yet, you might consider dipping your paw in. There are plenty of online communities out there, and even a few porn sites, to get you started. The costumes are a little expensive—ranging from a few hundred to a few thousand dollars, depending on how lifelike you want it to be—but you can always try making your own. Either way, just don't forget the SPH!

Once you've got your own costume, head to one of the many conventions that pop up around the country to meet other Fursuit Fetishists like yourself. And don't be surprised if you find a cute little dead-eyed fox "murring" at you. That's your cue to follow the fox up to his or her room. (You are totally getting some tail!)

PSYCHOLOGICAL ORIGINS

Many, though not all, Fursuit Fetishists identify themselves as Furries. But that name actually belongs to a pretty big tent, including people who are really into anthropomorphic animal drawings as well as those who are really into stuffed animals. In both camps, there are many who are just fascinated collectors, and then there are those who take it a step farther (Plushophilia, page 94; Schediaphilia, page 120). The sexually interested of the two groups intersect at the Fursuit Fetish. In one case, the fursuit can be seen as a sort of giant living teddy bear, and, in the other, as the closest possible substitute for actually embodying their "fursona."

Skeptical? Please be assured that *nobody* could make this stuff up.

CONSIDERATIONS

If you've never worn one of those costumes before, you should know that it can get very hot inside there. And oxygen is in rather short supply. Any strenuous physical activities you do while wearing the costume should be kept to short bursts.

Performers who wear such costumes for entertaining children are usually advised against taking off the head in front of the kids, as the sight of a half-person/half-animal may scar their fragile psyches. But in a Fursuit Fetish situation, that problem most likely wouldn't (and shouldn't) come up; you should probably just stay away from children altogether. Especially if your costume sports an SPH.

Of Note . . .

A Furpile is when a group of Fursuiters gather and press themselves together into a furry clump or literally pile on top of one another. What happens next? That's for you to find out. *Muurrrr . . .*

MUMMIFICATION FETISH

The enjoyment of an activity that has absolutely nothing to do with pyramids, ancient curses, or Boris Karloff.

USEFUL ACCOUTREMENTS

- plastic wrap
- elastic bandages
- duct tape
- breathing tube

THE FANTASY

In these moments, it's almost possible to believe he's still the same boy you met all those years ago after that fateful Bauhaus show. His face was so smooth and fresh. You can still see your fingers, nails polished black, encompassing his pale, gaunt, naked limbs, enveloping him tightly from head to toe in crimson material. It could have happened yesterday.

Staring at him now, propped up in the corner, his body hidden under so many layers of muslin, velvet, plastic wrap, and black duct tape, he could still be that same boy who handed you a blood red bed sheet, cut into ribbons, and some medical tape and said, "Put me in my death shroud." Sure, the package is a little thicker in the middle, but there's always that sense that, once you cut him open, anyone can climb out. Any*thing* can climb out. Even your past.

In these moments, it's easy to think these things. In large part because he can't talk.

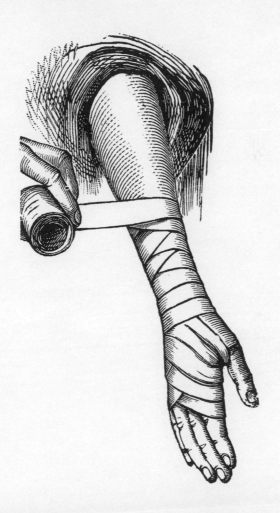

WHAT IS IT?

If you suffer from extreme claustrophobia or have difficulties with not being in control of a situation, then the Mummification Fetish is so totally *not* the fetish for you. (You might try something in a size 4 Shoe Fetish, page 98). However, if the idea of being bound so completely in plastic wrap and duct tape that you are unable to move or see gets you going, then read on. Your life is about to be changed.

First of all, you need to find somebody you can trust. Somebody who won't wrap you up and then get bored and leave you in a corner while they go watch TV. If you think you've found the right person, you can safely move on to the next step. Make yourself comfortable. You might want to use some sort of preliminary padding, such as towels or soft cloth, as base for your mummification. A blindfold is usually used as well. Then your partner should begin wrapping you in plastic wrap or bandages from head to toe. Several rolls may be necessary. (Important: If you plan on having your head wrapped for the full effect, and require oxygen to survive, consider the addition of a breathing tube.) Once that's done, have your partner follow with duct tape. That makes everything nice and tight and cozy.

Now that you're a proper mummee (note the preferred spelling), you're free to move on to the next part: standing around and doing nothing. If this is your first time as a mummee, you'll probably want to limit your session to fifteen minutes or so. Practiced Mummification Fetishists can go for hours. Some people like to have a hook wrapped into the bindings so that they can stand and do nothing more comfortably.

If you like, you may ask that certain areas of your body remain unwrapped. This will give your partner something to do while you stand around and do nothing.

PSYCHOLOGICAL ORIGINS

What can possibly be enjoyable about getting wrapped up like this? Well, many people describe the experience as similar to time spent in a sensory deprivation tank. You can't see anything. You can't move. Your hearing is impaired. It gives you time to relax with your thoughts and fully contemplate standing around and doing nothing. Some find the experience transcendent.

Or, from a more BDSM perspective, it's about as far as you can go as a submissive. You are entirely at the mercy of your partner, which many find to be highly erotic. And if you happen to suffer from claustrophobia, you may find mummification appealing precisely because being bound and out of control frightens you so much. In some people's brains, sex and fear are cross-wired.

COSTUMES & PLAY

CONSIDERATIONS

If not done properly, mummification can be extremely dangerous. While wrapped, the mummee can become extremely disoriented and may not be able to stand on his or her own. This leads to falling, and falling leads to bashing your head against the nightstand. This is almost never good. Therefore, your partner should stay with you at all times.

Also, as the mummee can't talk, a safe word per se is not really an option. You and your partner should instead establish a "safe grunt" or "safe moan" in case you start freaking out and need to get out. A pair of bandage scissors should be kept readily available at all times so that, if necessary, you can be free within seconds.

You and your partner should instead establish a "safe grunt" or "safe moan" in case you start freaking out and need to get out.

Of Note . . .

German writer Ulrich Haarbürste is indisputably the Ernest Hemingway of mummification fantasy fiction. He's built an impressive cult following for his stories about swaddling Roy Orbison in plastic wrap. In the stories—which can all be found on his website—the narrator and his pet terrapin, Jetta, happen upon the rock-and-roll legend time and again in various German locales (and, once, in outer space). In each scenario, the narrator is called upon to wrap Orbison up in "clingfilm," which he just happens to always have on hand. The genius of Haarbürste's words truly do speak for themselves:

"Roy Orbison unbuckles from his seat and floats out into the middle of the cabin, his black clothing billowing about him in the zero gravity like the folds of some black cloth manta ray . . . The clingfilm unfurls in languid arcs in the zero gravity and then girdles him gently as I spiral around him. Soon, Captain Roy Orbison of the Space Pioneers is completely wrapped in clingfilm. In all the infinite galaxies there is not a man as happy as I."

PETTICOAT DISCIPLINE
(ALSO PETTICOATING, PINAFORING)

The making of a man into a little girl.

USEFUL ACCOUTREMENTS

- petticoat
- pinafore
- ribbons
- stockings
- pretty little shoes
- psychological castration

THE FANTASY

Oh, just look at you. You look so adorable. Aren't you the sweetest thing? In that lovely dress and those sexy white stockings, with that fetching silk bow in your hair. Why, you're just the belle of the ball! Of course, you'll need to shave a little closer. It wouldn't be proper for such a darling vision as you to ruin it all by sporting a five-o'clock shadow.

And won't everybody be so happy to see you looking such a portrait of charm and delight. Their laughter will bring more red to your cheeks than the finest rouge could ever manage. But don't you cause a scene. Your shenanigans simply won't do tonight. It would be a shame if someone had to bend you over her knee and pull down your frilly pink panties to whack you a few times with a hairbrush, wouldn't it?

Suppose you're a proper society lady with a little boy who likes to dirty up his clothes by climbing trees, wrestling around in the mud, or shimmying under fences to sell government secrets to Bolshevik spies. You know, all those things that precocious lads do. How are you going to control a kid like that? Maybe you should try Petticoat Discipline, named for the ruffled, decorative underskirt that was once popular in women's fashions. Just dress your li'l rabble-rouser up in his sister's prettiest dress. (Don't forget the frilly panties and patent leather shoes!) Nothing will stop a boy from misbehaving like instilling the fear of being humiliated in front of a playmate or foreign agent.

Historically, Petticoat Discipline began as a form of punishment and control that goes back hundreds of years, but really had its heyday in the late-twentieth and early-nineteenth centuries. And it was not used solely for children. Young men found themselves in the cutest

little frocks well into their twenties, for such horrible of-
fenses as flirting with women or not being born a girl.
These men all went on to have very healthy sexual and
psychological lives.

Today, Petticoat Discipline exists primarily as a form
of BDSM, and it's usually quite voluntary on the male's
part. Adult men and women will often role-play scenarios
in which the man has misbehaved or must be degraded for
whatever reason. Your partner will "force" you to put on
women's clothing and will do your hair and makeup and
parade you around looking ever so pretty. Sometimes this
will be in the privacy of your bedroom. Sometimes in front
of friends. Sometimes out in public. Often, spanking or
whipping will be involved. But only if you've been really,
really bad.

PSYCHOLOGICAL ORIGINS

A fetish for Petticoating comes about in a number of different ways. If you experienced some form of Petticoating as
a child, its psychological scars may have become eroticized
for you. Or, if you are very masculine and controlling in
everyday life, it can serve as a respite from that rigidity.
Or you might simply like the way frilly things feel against
your thighs.

Although prolonged, enforced Petticoating in children often leads to lifelong, voluntary Transvestitism in adults, its BDSM variant is not considered a form of Transvestitism, because the aim is not gender transformation but humiliation. There's nothing humiliating about a woman dressing as a woman. But a man dressed as a woman is a different story. It's hard enough to get a guy to buy a pack of tampons at the drugstore.

Of Note . . .

Real-life involuntary Petticoat Discipline has been reported in several public schools within the past few years. In 2004, a Florida teacher made a five-year-old boy wear a yellow floral dress in front of his classmates because he was talking too much. And in 2001, a teacher in New York told a thirteen-year-old boy to wear a skirt, a bra, a wig, and high heels because he was behaving badly. When he refused, the teacher directed several other boys to get him into the clothes forcibly. (When did the U.S. educational system become so progressively BDSM? Hot!)

COSTUMES & PLAY

PONYPLAY
(ALSO PONYISM, PETPLAY)

A horse, a horse, a kinkiness for a horse.

USEFUL ACCOUTREMENTS

- bridle
- bit
- saddle
- kneepads
- eye-blinders
- riding crop
- salt lick

THE FANTASY

Is there anything finer than being cleaned and groomed by your owner after taking him for a long springtime ride through the park? His warm, soapy brush against your hide. The way he so gently combs through your thick blond mane. It is truly heavenly.

Every eye was on you this afternoon. Not a person failed to marvel at your perfect form as you trotted along with your owner sitting proudly up upon your back. Though speechless, their envious faces seemed to say, "My, what a breathtaking steed. And so well groomed! Her owner must love her very, very much."

And to think that for years, you dreamed of having a pony of your own. Who would have thought that *being* one could be so much better?

WHAT IS IT?

There are three main types of ponies: riding ponies, cart ponies, and show ponies. All three types of ponies have one thing in common: they're not ponies. A riding pony is usually a man (although it can be a woman) who acts the part of a horse and allows his "owner" to ride upon his back, either on all fours or two legs. A cart pony is a man or woman, acting as a horse, who pulls his or her "owner" around in a small riding cart. And a show pony, usually a woman (although it can be a man), acting as a horse, is groomed to be pretty, to have a graceful gait, and to be receptive to commands. The question you're probably asking yourself is: "What???" And that's a good question.

Ponyplay is an increasingly popular form of BDSM role-playing. Regular ordinary people, of their own free will, act as horses and let other people ride them around. And, in some cases, they'll spend thousands of dollars to do so. Special fetish shops sell all kinds of Ponyplay accessories and costumes, including saddles, reins, riding crops, leather bits, eye-blinders, and full head harnesses. If you really want to equinomorphize yourself, you can buy things like hoof-shaped boots, arm extensions with hooves, and butt plug–tail combos. (Because you gotta have a tail, right?) Oftentimes, pony gear will very much resemble bondage gear: leather corsets, metal rings, exposed breasts and genitalia, etc. Sometimes a pony will go completely nude, save for his or her bit and reins.

Ponyplay is pretty open-ended, except for a few general rules. A pony does not talk about Ponyplay during Ponyplay. In fact, a pony does not talk *at all*. (No one can talk to a horse, of course.) A pony does not use his or her arms during Ponyplay, unless he or she is an all-fours riding pony (in which case they're not arms anyway, they're front legs). A pony does not break character during Ponyplay. Beyond that, Ponyplay consists of whatever works best for everyone concerned. Ponies and owners can just have fun riding around. The owner can spend time grooming the pony, whatever that might entail. Or they can engage in hot pony/owner sex.

PSYCHOLOGICAL ORIGINS

Why would a person allow his or herself to be treated as an animal? Simple answer: for fun. Complex answer: for complex fun. Ponyplay is basically another form of role-playing and BDSM, but with a few quirks. Some people enjoy the sexual charge of willful humiliation (or, in the case of the owner, allowed humiliation). Other people don't find anything humiliating in playing the part of a noble steed.

One interesting aspect of Ponyplay—an important way in which it differs from most BDSM games—is that the pony is respected and cared for by the owner. While in a more "normal" bondage situation, the dominant mistress or master may act cruelly toward the submissive slave, in Ponyplay, the dominant owner treats the submissive pony as he or she would a real horse. A pony isn't a slave to an owner any more than a real horse is a slave to its rider; if you don't treat your horse kindly, you're likely to get bucked off. It's quite possible that most fans of Ponyplay enjoy the dominant/submissive aspects of BDSM, but not so much the cruelty aspects of it.

Or, maybe one of the people involved was that kinda pretty but vaguely creepy girl from junior high. You know, the one who drew pictures of horses all over her book covers? What was her deal, anyway?

If you don't treat your horse kindly, you're likely to get bucked off.

Safety is a necessity in Ponyplay, especially if you're a 120-pound ponygirl carrying a 200-pound male owner around on your back. Human spines were not built for that kind of use. Often, a trainer is employed to, well, train the pony in the proper ways to walk, behave, whinny, and accept orders. Training may involve cardiovascular exercise and weightlifting. And since many ponies have their arms restrained behind their backs, learning proper balance is important in preventing injuries. It would be a real shame if your pretty little pony broke its leg on a rocky country road and you had to put it down.

Of Note . . .

Ponyplay is sometimes referred to as the Aristotelian Perversion. It is widely believed that the Greek philosopher was a big fan of riding his wife around on his back. (As Plato pointed out, it totally makes sense for him when you think about it.)

COSTUMES & PLAY

ROBOFETISH
(ALSO ANDROIDISM, TECHNOSEXUALITY, TECHNOFET, ASFR)

The desire to have sexual relations with an unfeeling automaton. A robot, not a DMV employee.

USEFUL ACCOUTREMENTS

- robot costume
- remote control
- power cable

THE FANTASY

Everybody keeps talking about how our new robot overlords are so terrible. Yeah, yeah, yeah, they do keep disintegrating people with their eye-socket death-rays. And it probably would suck to get crushed beneath their massive metallic treads.

But c'mon, that one over there—the one who just exploded the Capitol Building with his sonic destructo-beam? He's so *cute*. So hard, and strong, and shiny.

I bet he works out.

One might imagine that the Robofetish—a sexual attraction toward or concerning robots—would have arisen only in the past couple decades, when robots actually started to exist, but that would be an information error. Please reboot and install the following information: One of the first major robots of pop culture was Hel, the mechanical woman built by the scientist Rotwang in Fritz Lang's *Metropolis*. But Hel shares many similarities with the monster in Mary Shelley's *Frankenstein*, and the monster was in turn heavily based upon Jewish folklore tales of golems, creatures built from mud and animated by God's true name. Some people even read the Bible's book of Genesis as the first golem tale, since God shapes Adam from dust before breathing life into him. The most widely regarded Classical origin to the Robofetish, though, is the very erotic Greek myth of Pygmalion (see Agalmatophilia, page 154).

Technological advances have, in more ways than one, helped Robofetishism explode in recent years, when a Robofetishist who called himself Robotdoll started an Internet newsgroup called *alt.sex.fetish.robots*. People who had felt all alone in their getting off on animatronic dolls and publicity stills of C-3PO were suddenly part of a community. The newsgroup is now gone—a victim of spambots, ironically—but its influences are legion. Today, you'd need a high-performance multi-core processor (or something similarly techno-sounding, but which actually makes sense) to count all the ASFR-influenced websites.

But you don't care about any of that, do you? You want to read about people wearing shiny silver suits with fake data-input buttons sewn on and saying things like "System overload! System overload!" while having electro-sex, right? Well, that's certainly a part of it. So, you can download porn digitally manipulated to make it look like sections of flesh have been pulled away, exposing the circuitry beneath, or you can dress up and have fun. Walk mechanically around the bedroom and ask your master or mistress for instructions in a clipped monotone. Or break-dance the horizontal Robot with hydraulic pelvic thrusts until your battery is discharged and you're forced to power down.

While some Robofetishists would jump at the chance to have actual sex with an actual robot, technology has not yet caught up with the fetish. Others, however, have no interest in sleeping with an actual machine. For them, it's simply enjoyable role-playing. In fact, some don't want anything to do with the modern concept of robots, preferring to fill their fantasy life with the herky-jerkier clockwork dolls and steam-powered machines of the past. (Some people are such traditionalists.)

PSYCHOLOGICAL ORIGINS

Robofetishism shares many similarities with other BDSM-based fetishes. There is an inherent domination/submission quality to the fantasy—after all, a robot is at the mercy of its programmer or owner. Philosopher Erich Fromm, for his part, blames the isolation of modern living: "Sexuality becomes a technical skill (the 'love machine'), feelings are flattened . . . and whatever love and tenderness man has is directed towards machines and gadgets." In all fairness, though, he wrote that back in the early '70s, before robots started looking all hot.

CONSIDERATIONS

If you're gonna have sex with a robot, make certain it's a good robot, and not one bent on world domination. Because those robots are not programmed to care about your needs. And you may end up disintegrated.

Of Note . . .

By international law, it is illegal to write more than three paragraphs about robots without mentioning science-fiction writer Isaac Asimov. This book is now in compliance with TechnoLit Directive #3.

SUPERHERO FETISH

The pursuit of truth, justice, and a huge erection.

USEFUL ACCOUTREMENTS

- stash of comic books
- spandex (or Lycra) bodysuit
- cape
- mask
- secret identity
- rope (or lariat, preferably gold)
- Kryptonite (real or synthesized)
- awkward adolescence

THE FANTASY

Aha! You finally have her! Using your super tracking skills, you've managed to find the evil Cobrawoman here in her secret volcano base of operations. It was a long and exhausting battle, but, utilizing your supreme speed and ultra-dexterity, you've managed to tear the madwoman's Reptillo-Suit—from which she derives her unearthly powers—from her lean and supple body. Now, she looks up at you, uncostumed, helpless. You should have no problem restraining her, nude and bound, until the police arrive.

But—oh no!—what's this? Have you forgotten her Sonic Charm Machine? Its acoustic hypnosis effects course through your brain. You cannot help yourself! Your hand reaches down against your will. Cobrawoman hisses with pleasure as you unfasten the belt on your Spandex unitard.

The poor citizens of your town will die in a fiery explosion for certain. But some sacrifices are unavoidable.

WHAT IS IT?

Somewhere, deep in the bowels of Suburbia, Hew-Munn-Gus—jaded regional manager by day, criminal mastermind by night—is holding aloft a blue and silver spandex costume, scheming desperately to get his wife to climb into it and assume her alter-ego: ElectroWoman. What fiendish plans does he have in store for the superheroine? Will they include the Handcuffs of Submission . . . again? Will the torture of nipple pinching break her will as quickly as it did last Wednesday, or will she at least *pretend* to resist his evil wiles for a few minutes? And will they keep it quiet enough so as not to alert their teenaged son, Virgin Lad, who is, at this very moment, in his bedroom downloading nudie pictures from Google Images, trying to figure out which one he can most easily manipulate in Photoshop to make it look like Rogue from the X-Men is stepping out of the shower?

If you're not into dress-up, there is an easier way to go about your Superhero Fetish: remain a passive observer and simply view the myriad websites in which people act out, illustrate, or photo-manipulate (mostly female) superheroes in various poses and life-threatening situations. From these sites, you might assume that every superhero is completely worthless, because they're all either mugging for the camera in cheesecake poses or getting beaten down and tied up—their costumes torn to pieces—by supervillains who look like your next door neighbor.

PSYCHOLOGICAL ORIGINS

Considering that so many sexual proclivities have their basis in childhood memories, it doesn't take an evil genius to figure out how an adolescence spent reading stories about well toned, misunderstood heroes in formfitting costumes who continually find themselves in life-threatening situations might translate easily into something like this.

If you do feel the need for further research, please see practically any issue of *Wonder Woman*. (With her golden lariat of truth and bad habit of allowing herself to be hog-tied by her enemies, it's practically a how-to manual for BDSM.)

CONSIDERATIONS

The Superhero Fetish is pretty harmless, assuming all parties are consenting and rational boundaries are respected. Just like in any other form of BDSM, if you're going to be tying anyone up with power-draining yarn or similar materials, it's a good idea to set safe words beforehand.

> ## *Of Note . . .*
>
> What's that online? Is it a bird rendered helpless by toxic gas? Is it a plane pinned to the ground by tight cord? No, it's Super Becca, queen of the online super-damsels-in-distress! She may not be adept at leaping tall buildings or rudimentary feats of video production, but, in her tight, low-cut, primary-colored costumes, the forty-nine-year-old North Carolina entrepreneur looks good enough, bound and gagged, to keep throngs of Superhero Fetishists returning to her website day after day.

VORAREPHILIA
(ALSO VORAPHILIA, VORE, PHAGOPHILIA)

The feeling that people who eat people are the luckiest people.

USEFUL ACCOUTREMENTS

- human-sized roasting pan
- cooking twine
- herbs
- spices
- prctend oven
- anal thermometer

THE FANTASY

You really hope she put out the good dishes this time. And the candles. And the cloth napkins—somehow those just complete the experience, make it feel like the meal deserves everyone's full attention.

You can barely contain your excitement as you head into the kitchen, breathing in the warm smells of her culinary efforts . . . creamy garlic mashed potatoes . . . tangy cranberry chutney . . . soft, yeasty buttered rolls . . . But there's something missing. Something very important. You're unable to make out anything that smells like—well, like a main course.

"Honey," you ask, a hopeful smile creeping across your face, "what's for dinner?"

"Why, I've made your favorite," comes her coy response. "*You.*"

WHAT IS IT?

Did you know that just about everybody on Earth eats on at least a semi-regular basis? That's a fact. You can look it up. It's really become all the rage. Almost as popular as sex. Eating has become so popular, in fact, that there's a growing number of people who opt to combine their twin passions for eating and sexing and satisfy both urges simultaneously with a little thing called Vorarephilia. This is the sexual excitement found in eating or imagining yourself being eaten. Consumed. Chewed up, swallowed, and allowed to pass through the digestive tract, thereby providing nourishment to the consumer. Granted, most Vorarephiliacs probably don't carry the fantasy that far, but if there's one thing you should carry away from this book, it's that one should never underestimate the human sexual appetite.

Because people generally (with some notable exceptions—Zoophilia, page 146; Entomophilia, page 142) prefer to have sex with other people, Vorarephilia tends to keep its focus on eating other people. But not necessarily. The fantastic thing about Vorarephilia, as with sex in general, is that you can have it your way. If you and your partner want to role-play gutting, roasting, and carving one another, that's fine. If you'd prefer to skip past all the more graphic aspects of food preparation and just dress up in pastrami sandwich costumes, that's fine too. If you want to seriously embody the essence of a bowl of Pad Thai for several hours, that, as well, is fine. And once it comes to the "eating" part, you can just let your imagination soar. There are all kinds of things you can do with body parts and mouths.

Vorarephilia is not necessarily related to Sitophilia (page 102)—the use of actual foods in sex—but the two may very easily be blended (or frappéd) together.

PSYCHOLOGICAL ORIGINS

Vorarephilia is a relatively new item on the fetish menu, so it hasn't been studied to any great degree. However, it is a form of BDSM, usually with the "eater" taking the dominant role and the "food" taking the submissive, so, like Forniphilia (page 162), it's most likely satisfying some need to objectify or be objectified.

Its origins are likely to be found somewhere in childhood. Perhaps in exposure to bedtime stories that involve characters being consumed, such as *The Gingerbread Man*, *Jack and the Beanstalk*, or *The Silence of the Lambs*. Or perhaps your first lover bore an uncanny olfactory resemblance to *Foie Gras d'Oie*.

When playtime is over,
everyone should be able to
carry on with his or her normal
non-food existences.

CONSIDERATIONS

Do not actually eat anybody! Anthropophagy, or genuine
cannibalism, is illegal, illegal, illegal. And in some states,
it's *highly* illegal. Unless you're a member of a Uruguayan
Rugby team trapped in the Andes, eating other human
beings is unacceptable behavior, regardless of your fantasies—sexual, gastronomic, whatever. Armin Meiwes, the
infamous German internet cannibal/computer geek, was
sentenced to life in prison for killing and eating Bernd
Jürgen Armando Brandes, a man who had responded to
an online personal ad proposing such a relationship. And
that was consensual. (Although, some argue that the very
act of consenting to such a proposition shows that you're
psychologically incapable of actually consenting to such a
proposition. Kind of a Catch 222° F.)

What you have to remember is this: Sexual fantasies are sexual fantasies. When playtime is over, everyone should be able to carry on with his or her normal non-food existences. Because once you're eaten in real life, you don't ever get to go back and experience that again. And you probably didn't get to experience it the first time, since you were already cleaned and cooked.

Of Note . . .

Don't forget that you pretend are what you pretend eat. If you're going to pretend eat a girl who's dressed up as a jelly doughnut, she's going to pretend go right to your ass. And if you keep pretend filling up on pretend jelly doughnut girls, you might find yourself not so attractive to pretend jelly doughnut girls in the future. Sure, a pretend jelly doughnut girl is fine from time to time, but how about a little pretend sushi girl? And would it kill you to pretend eat a pretend spinach salad girl every now and then?

WET & MESSY FETISH
(ALSO SPLOSH, WAM)

The understanding that love can be messy. And wet. And squishy.

USEFUL ACCOUTREMENTS

- O pistachio pudding
- O Hollandaise sauce
- O garlic mayonnaise
- O Thousand Island salad dressing
- O New England clam chowder

THE FANTASY

This is going to be the most romantic dinner ever! Your girlfriend is going to be so surprised. Let's just make sure everything's ready for when she comes in. Okay, for an appetizer, there's a ten-gallon pot of lukewarm beef barley soup sitting precariously on the edge of that bookshelf by the front door. Excellent. For the main course, a barrel of spaghetti and meatballs propped up on that rickety stepladder. Perfect! Of course, you'll need red wine. The two or three gallons you've got in that slop bucket dangling from the ceiling and attached to that trip wire ought to be enough. And, for dessert, a washbasin full of hot fudge sundae over there on the floor. Nice!

Here she comes, you can hear her heels clicking on the hallway floor. Sounds like she dressed up for the occasion. Let's hope she's wearing her finest, most expensive dining attire. Something delicate, something dry-clean-only, something . . . Yes! She wore white!

WHAT IS IT?

If you've ever had sex, or know anybody who's ever had sex, then you probably know that it can get a little wet and kinda messy. Especially toward the end. (A note to any monks or otherwise abstinent folks out there: Sex can be a little messy. Now, please put this book down immediately and go back to studying.) However, there's a kind of sex that takes messiness to a whole new level: The Wet and Messy Fetish.

Take a bathtub full of cottage cheese, a pretty girl, and a prom dress. Now put the pretty girl in the prom dress and then put them both in the bathtub with the cottage cheese. Then take pictures of the whole thing and post them on the Internet. Congratulations! You've just made a Splosher's day. "Splosher" is what many Wet and Messy Fetish aficionados call themselves. And while different Sploshers like various kinds of wet and specific kinds of messy, in general, they like things that are wet and messy.

Very often the messiness is edible (melted chocolate, mashed potatoes, tapioca pudding, strawberry cake batter), but it can also be non-edible (silver paint, shaving cream, mud) or quasi-edible (shepherd's pie). Indeed, pies seem to be very popular. Sploshers enjoy watching people—usually, but not always, women—pied in the face, pied in the breasts, pied in the pie, or simply sitting down on a nice squishy chocolate cream pie. Luckily for Splosh models, there's a whole subset of Splosh fans who enjoy the wet without the messy, so at least they get to rinse off.

As fetishes go, Wet and Messy might be wet and messy, but it's rarely very *dirty*. Obviously, sex does enter into some Splosh porn, but not as often as you might think. Most of the Splosh fodder available online takes things only to the point where the model is covered head-to-toe in goo. Of course, if you and your partner want to engage in Wet and Messy play at home, you can take it as far as you like. But you should probably throw down a tarp first.

PSYCHOLOGICAL ORIGINS

Like Coulrophilia (page 158), which also makes generous use of pies, one of the big attractions of the Wet and Messy Fetish is that it's goofy and fun—a much less serious take on sexuality than is often found in porn or fetish play. It's kind of hard to keep a straight face and act solemnly passionate when you're chasing down a half-naked girl with a bucket of blueberry pie filling above your head.

But why so gooey? There are a zillion possible answers, depending on who you're asking, but part of it is probably that, even though it's all done in slap-sticky fun, there's an element of BDSM involved. Being covered by your partner in slime, while probably pretty fun, is still something of a defilement.

CONSIDERATIONS

Keep in mind that people's bodies are vulnerable. If you or your partner gets into a tub filled with chocolate sauce, some of that chocolate sauce is going to wind up in unpleasant places. Sugary materials may encourage the growth of yeast and bacteria, leading to infections. So when finished, just make certain you clean your insides as well as you clean your outsides.

APPENDIX: ASSORTED FETISHES & FIXATIONS

Abasiophilia: The urge to fondle the metal workings of orthopedic appliances.

Acousticophilia: The sexual arousal awakened by that obnoxious car alarm outside your apartment.

Amaurophilia: The sexual ecstasy of being unable to see.

Apodysophilia/Exhibitionism: The desire to show your genitalia to unsuspecting strangers.

Aquaphilia: The desire to get down underwater.

Aretifism: The sexual attraction to people who are without footwear.

Asphyxiophilia: The sexual delight associated with being unable to breathe.

Autogynephilia: The enjoyment a man receives from fantasizing about himself as a woman.

Celebriphilia: The pathological desire to have sex with a celebrity—whichever one's handy.

Coprolalia: The need to talk really, shockingly filthily to get off.

Faunoiphilia: The fulfillment found in watching two animals do it like a couple of animals.

Gerontophilia: The belief that old people are *hot*.

Haematophilia/Hematolagnia: The sexual attraction to blood.

Harpaxophilia: The arousal received from getting mugged.

Hybristophilia: The sexual attraction to criminals.

Katoptronophilia: The desire to get it on in front of a mirror.

Lust murder: The sexual pleasure in stone-cold murdering someone.

Maiesiophilia: The desire to get busy with a pregnant woman.

Mysophilia: The love of filth.

Phalloorchoalgolagnia: The desire to have electrodes strapped to your testicles.

Pyrophilia: The sexual penchant for fire.

Salirophilia: The enjoyment of consuming another person's sweat.

Somnophilia: The wanting to sleep with people who are sleeping.

Stigmatophilia: The sexual pleasure derived from jabbing objects into one's own body.

Teratophilia: The attraction to people who are deformed.

Transvestic Fetishism: The predilection toward guys who have a predilection toward dressing up as girls.

Voyeurism: The sexual excitement of watching other people who are naked or engaged in sex.

Xenophilia: The sexual attraction to foreigners, or possibly aliens.

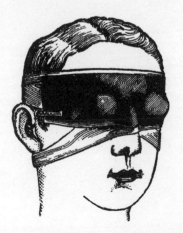

ACKNOWLEDGMENTS

I've said it before: There are so many people I would like to thank that the list itself could be published separately as *The Obsessive-Compulsive Author's Pocket Guide to People I'd Like to Acknowledge Here in the Acknowledgments*. However, I've been advised that that book wouldn't sell very well. So, here, unfortunately, is an extremely abridged version:

. . . Susan DiClaudio, Dennis DiClaudio, Sr., Denelle DiClaudio, Anthony DiClaudio, Diandra DiClaudio, Carmen Panarello, Anthony DiMaggio, Ray DiClaudio, and my entire family . . .

. . . Amy Wideman and all the folks at becker&mayer! . . .

. . . Yelena Gitlin, Colin Dickerman, Benjamin Adams, and everyone at Bloomsbury USA . . .

. . . Paula Balzer . . .

. . . Suzanne Lanza, for her extreme patience . . .

. . . and every one of my friends who would probably rather not have their names included in a book alongside such topics as Klismaphilia and Eproctophilia (even though you know they're totally into it).

Thank you all!